A SHERPA NAMED ZOI

HOW TO WALK THROUGH GRIEF AND LIVE WITH INTENTION

Eric Hodgdon

Dedicated to you, my sweet Zoi.

I love you, always and forever.

—Dad

ISBN-13: 9781973265870

Published by

Eric Hodgdon
39 Rockhill Street
Norwood, MA 02062
Website: EricHodgdon.com

For bulk purchases and speaking engagements, contact:

Eric Hodgdon
39 Rockhill Street
Norwood, MA 02062
508-878-3549
eric@erichodgdon.com

Because of the dynamic nature of the Internet, web addresses or links contained in this book may have changed since publication and may no longer be valid.

The author of this book does not dispense medical, legal, or psychological advice, nor does he suggest any technique as a form of treatment for medical, physical, or emotional problems. Always consult the appropriate professional. Your use of the information in this book for yourself is your responsibility; you are responsible for the actions and outcomes resulting in the use of the information contained herein. The author assumes no responsibility or liability for the outcome of those actions.

Editor: Mark Tompkins

Layout/Cover/Illustrations: Eric Hodgdon, Everett O'Keefe

TABLE OF CONTENTS

INTRODUCTION

Why this book?

Death may take your loved one's life, but it doesn't have to take yours.

"I don't feel like I'm ever going to feel better." I hear this all the time when talking to someone about loss. Typically, it's around their own experience. Or, at the very least, someone close to them that they want to help — but don't know how to. Death is one of the most difficult and painful life experiences to work through. The thing is, this isn't our ancestors' experience with death and grief. In fact, in the last 75 years, we've seen a huge shift in how people process grief.

What we see today are thousands of people who try to cope through a loss, and it challenges them immensely. They can't see past their own sadness and therefore cannot begin to fathom entering a state of resilience. Here's the thing:, we will all experience death in our lives at some point. Every year in the U.S. alone, approximately 2,500,000 people die. But what about the tens of millions of people who are affected by a death and struggle to make sense of it, to make peace and make their future brighter? It's a struggle that gripped me for a long time. Maybe it's gripping you too? Maybe you're stuck and don't know how to smile again, to find those better days? The good news is, those better days ARE possible.

Two paths exist

On our journey, I believe there are two paths that exist — a choice is made for either:

Path One: We are stuck and can't see a way through the pain and the fog of the loss. Sometimes we are there for a short period of time. Or we stay there indefinitely — pitching a tent at Camp "This Sucks."

Path Two: We make peace with the loss, find gratitude for what is and continue to move along our journey and into a state of resilience to thrive and celebrate the life of the person (or people) we've lost, eventually arriving at Camp "Ever Bright."

Personally, I choose to take Path Two. And with guidance, this path is possible for you too! Here is the rub: no one is coming to take that journey on Path Two for you. In this book I will show you how to take that journey, and I will walk it with you, but I can't walk it for you.

There are a lot of wonderful organizations, therapists and groups out there that help with grief and loss. Sometimes there is just so much out there to choose from, we don't know where to turn, except inward — shades drawn, in bed, crying. Sometimes for a few hours, sometimes for a few months. And for some people, for the rest of their lives. For this very reason, and from what I've seen on my own journey, I decided to fight for my family and friends to find the pathway back to better days. And I extend that fight for your better days, your resilience as well.

As I moved through my struggle of grief and into a state of resilience, I steered clear of what I felt was a detriment to my healing and chose to explore what did matter to me in this process. That's why I wrote this book.

Why is death so different for us today?

Death has been part of life since the beginning of time. For thousands of years, through ceremonies, rituals and gatherings, death was both processed together and celebrated as a rite of passage — in the clan. In this age of smartphones and social media, "togetherness" is just one text or post away. We do come together for the wake, the funeral and the reception. But, invariably, that gathering of family and friends dissipates after a very short period of time. There is no "clan," so to speak, in our world. We go back to our lives and in this age of instant gratification, the expectation is that we "get over it" as soon as possible. Or at the very least, we are asked/told to do so. Life does go on, but finding resilience in the midst of loss today requires a renewed approach. But there lacks an understanding of what comes next. For most of us, we try to deal with grief and loss individually. We aren't wired for that. We are wired to process death together.

In this book, I'll show you how Path One — that of being stuck — can lead toward more isolation and remaining at Camp "This Sucks." And personally, I didn't want that for myself. I chose to thrive and to live into a greater purpose for my life and go for Camp "Ever Bright." If any of this resonates with you, keep reading.

Answering the question of why we are here, what our purpose is, and why we should keep going, is the direction of this book. To do that, I am going to be very open about what overcoming loss means:

- To you individually, trying to work through a loss;
- To your friends and family, who are wondering how they can step in and help;

- To your co-workers, who may not know how to help or what to say to you in your time of grief;
- To everyone else, who may want to know what processing grief really means to the person going through it.

The backpack of tools you find here, you won't find in any support group. It's exactly the set of tools that we can and should take with us as we move along in this journey, trekking toward that state of resilience.

What this book is all about

The concept of this book is simple:

If you are someone who has lost a loved one to death — at any age — you are already pre-wired and have everything inside of you to move through the loss. I will help you unlock these tools.

If you know someone who has lost a loved one and you see that they need help, but don't know what to do for them, I will help you figure out how to help them.

Your Sherpa along this journey

Through story and experience, this book will guide you on how to reconnect with yourself. We will work to accept that our loved ones are in fact OK, so as to give you a sense of peace. We will help you work through the struggles, to stand back up after getting knocked down, and to open up the space to move into a resilient life.

To do that, I've broken this book up into four parts. While any of the four parts can be helpful to you, I recommend reading from start to finish so as to maximize your understanding of this journey back to better days, as it relates to both you and your experience of loss.

Part I, "All Along the Journey," contains origin stories for me and several others whom I have come to know in my life. In this section, we'll take a journey through birth, coming of age, growing into adulthood, parenthood and experiences with death — all along the journey. We'll also look at the various coping mechanisms that were at play for all of us in these life-changing events.

Part II, "A Deep Breath," focuses on functioning through the immediacy of a death and then exploring the questions that we ask most. For some of us, these questions swirl around us so much they cause us to remain stuck, where we simply can't move on. Questions like:

- Did I do enough for them?
- How am I going to move on?
- Will I ever feel better?

Part III, "Coming Out of the Fog," gives us the three best 'F' words as we walk through the grief and raise our frequency to see the beauty in life. They are: Framing your mindset, to go from thinking 'Why did this happen to me," to 'Why is this happening for me'; Function with intention — doing the things in your life that make your heart sing; and finally, Formation of your core values, doing that which brings energy and direction to your life.

Part IV, "Thriving": When we work toward this, new opportunities present themselves in our lives. You find and live into your greater purpose and find beautiful meaning in your days. You still experience the pain of the loss, and setbacks in life, but instead of being knocked down fully, you only get bumped and stay upright.

Who this book is for

A Sherpa Named Zoi is for anyone who needs guidance through loss, through the storm, to help come out of the fog, and who wants to live in a state of resilience for themselves and their family and who ultimately wants to help others to do the same.

There is no timeline for grief, and you don't have to be within any age or group to change your life in this way. When you take your last breath on this earth, do you want to take a deep breath and know that you did everything possible, or will it be a small, short breath, full of regret for the things not done?

"It's been several years and my aunt is still not over the death of her son," says my friend Kofi Jones. "She doesn't feel like there will ever be a day when she will feel like she can smile or be happy again. I wish I could help her."

I wrote this book for anyone who has experienced loss, whether it be personal or if you know someone who has lost a loved one. It does not matter if that loss came to you two days ago, or 20 years ago; overcoming loss IS possible and we are wired to be resilient. It's just stepping onto the path to get started that can be difficult. Even if you haven't experienced loss and you need to locate your greater purpose, this book is for you. Loss is loss and setbacks in life are an excellent launching pad to not only build resilience, but also to accelerate your life in directions that may not even seem possible now.

A Sherpa Named Zoi is also for anyone who has yet to experience loss and would like to know how to navigate the difficult days, months and sometimes years ahead, from those who have done so already. It may eventually serve to help you speak with others who have experienced loss. To truly be there for someone who has suffered loss, and in the capacity in which they need support, is huge. Silence and not knowing what to say are always awkward, especially when ALL you want to do is help. What brings us together here is the mutual desire to navigate loss and to thrive in life.

What this book is not

A Sherpa Named Zoi will not fix anything for you. Only you can take the journey, and only you can find those better days. Please do not look outside of your own pre-wired nature to let the path just come to you. While there are no timelines for working through grief, and as much as we may want to not feel this pain even one more second, there are no shortcuts. "The obstacle is the path," in the words of Buddha.

This grief "process" is exactly that, a process. Just as it was a process to learn and grow in life, so too is this process to grow and learn in the presence of death. "Life is a journey that must be traveled no matter how bad the roads and accommodations." — Oliver Goldsmith.

Viewing this difficult journey as something that will enhance and transform your life is not only one of the BEST gifts that you can give to yourself in the light of a loss, but also one of the BEST things you can do to honor the person that you have lost.

My promise to you

When you finish this book, you will be informed of a new way of thinking that will take you to new levels of living your life, especially after experiencing a deep loss. You will have the tools to help you not just survive your grief and struggle, but thrive because of it. Tools to help you carry on in your healing journey that NO ONE else is talking about — not in grief counseling groups, not in family settings, not even among friends who want to help you.

I'm hoping to make an impact in your life — to reopen your eyes as to why you were born in the first place — and you may even be pissed off with some of the things that I'm going to say in this book. But that's the point: if it doesn't impact you, you would have no impetus to take that first step on the journey toward thriving and seeing the beauty in life again. There is light on the other side of the fog you are in, and it will guide you through. I want this book to be that light and the hope.

I'm going to help you answer the questions that you most want answered when it comes to loss. These are the questions that you ask yourself daily, and even sometimes when you are jolted awake by a dream or memory of the person you lost. You are alive — and they aren't any more. I know, because I've experienced those moments too.

And while I'm honest about this process of fighting for better days, this book is not going to feed any negative narratives about death in today's society. Instead it will introduce positive disruptors for growth and resilience for you and countless others around you.

If you'll open your mind and take these gifts and tools to heart, and apply them toward a long-term goal of both fighting for and reaching better days, you will vastly reduce the time it takes to not only get back on your feet and actually fight for your own better days, but also to fight for those around you to find their better days, too.

Anyone who promises that they have the "cure-all" for loss, or that they can "get you back to feeling normal in a couple of weeks" is blowing smoke up your ass. But the chance to grow into a better life, bypassing any supposed shortcuts, with the knowledge that we are here for a bigger purpose than to just exist — doing all of this with the goal of seeing better days is exactly what you deserve, and what you will reach.

Let's fight for better days, together!

PART I

ALL ALONG THE JOURNEY

"The journey of a thousand miles begins with one step."

— Lao Tzu

1.

Pathways

When I was 10 years old I used to go exploring in the woods of Brunswick, Maine by myself. I could get lost in nature for hours at a time, and often did. We had 25 acres of untouched, wooded property, complete with paths that enveloped our neighborhood like veins. Some of this untouched land was owned by a church, but a developer owned most of it. Wild blueberries, wild blackberries and white pine trees were everywhere. Although I walked the paths alone most of the time, I never felt alone. To me, it provided a gold mine of adventure. I had no map, but I felt connected and sometimes got lost on purpose.

For quite some time, everything was copacetic. We didn't bother the developer in any way and he didn't care if us kids were playing on his land. But that unspoken treaty between us was broken one spring morning when I heard the buzzing of chainsaws and the sounds of diesel engines from several bulldozers. I was in denial about what was happening, because I believed we would always have this land to ourselves. I never imagined that we would lose any of it. Over the years, inevitably, the developer sold more chunks of that land — restricting us kids to a smaller and smaller area to explore and play in. As I grew into my teens, I traversed the shrinking area of the paths less and less. And by the time I turned 18, instead of being overtaken by weeds, most of the paths were overtaken by streets, and then by new homes.

2

Life touches everyone

I met my very best friend Scott in fourth grade. I had to make up a prior assignment that I had missed the previous day because I was sick at home. Scott came in as a new student, and since I was the only kid in the classroom at the time, the teacher asked me to show Scott around. After recess, when everyone came back into the classroom, they were introduced to Scott. But it really wasn't until Scott's family moved into our neighborhood a few years later that our friendship got stronger.

I grew up in the Seventies and Eighties. My dad, Walt, was a Navy pilot and my mom, Kris, worked as a secretary for an architect. My sister, Holly, was navigating junior high school. When it was warm outside, my dad would mostly work in our garage on the weekends, either tinkering with Mom's 1970 Oldsmobile Vista Cruiser, or building/repairing something. The garage was his "man cave." Out there he was always dressed in an old, worn-out olive green Navy flight suit. An old AM/FM radio sat on the workbench at the back of the garage and he had the dial set on an easy listening station while he worked his magic in the cave. I think I saw more of my dad's legs protruding out from beneath a car than him actually standing up. If he was taking on a day-long project with one of the cars, I would often crawl under at various times to see what he was doing. And like most kids who know nothing about tools at 10, he would ask me to get a specific socket. I'd usually get it wrong a few times before I got it right. But really to help out, I would bring Dad a Diet Pepsi with ice without him asking. He always acknowledged that as being the best drink he had ever tasted. I could see it in his face. I knew at the end of the day when the project was done, I had successfully helped Dad.

One Saturday morning, mid-November 1980, we had some unusually warm weather. Dad was getting the garage cleaned up and ready for the winter weather that was fast approaching. I was with him when I heard the phone ring. I ran, picked it up, and it was my grandmother, my dad's mother. She didn't call us much, but I was surprised and happily said "Hi Nana!" She quickly asked to speak to my dad. He came inside and we both sat at the kitchen table for a few minutes while he just listened. He muttered only a few words and I looked while his face went blank. When he hung up, I asked what Nana wanted. He simply said, "My dad died." He just sat there stunned and didn't say anything else. I didn't know what to say either. While I understood the words that he just said to me, this was new and I wasn't sure what I was feeling. When my mom and Holly got home from their morning out running errands, I ran out and told them. By then, it had sunk in and Dad was very upset and crying. Mom went into prep mode and was focused on making calls, packing and getting things together to head down to the Boston area with my dad that night. Holly was upset too. All I remember was that this was an odd feeling at 10 years old. In my effort to try and comfort Dad I said, "Please tell Grampa Milty I said 'Hi.'" I fully knew he was dead, but out of sadness Dad said to me, "I can't...you don't understand."

As Scott and I grew up, our friendship grew too. It ebbed and flowed as most friendships do. We had periods of peace and periods of fighting, like brothers would. We too spent time in the same woods that surrounded our neighborhood. When we were 12, we were walking the paths one day with our BB guns and we started to argue and fight about something that only a 12-year-old mind could find significant. We started to get further away from each other, and from a good distance apart we began to shoot in each other's direction, not taking any time to aim. Being much faster on foot than Scott, I ran out of the woods across the street to a newly framed house that was being built, and I hid around back. We continued our battle, albeit playfully pissed at each other. We could hear BBs bouncing off the wood of the house frame. Getting a little braver, I made my way to the front corner of the house, held the gun and reached around the corner and blindly shot in the direction I thought Scott was in.

I heard him scream in pain. I came running up to see him holding his left eye and yelling that it hurt. Oh, shit! Fight over! I just shot my best friend's eye out! He couldn't open his eye or determine if the BB was inside or not. We were both scared that something bad happened to his eye. Then the pain turned to panic when Scott became more worried about being in trouble than being hurt. Hell, we both were. So we concocted a story that we were shooting at a milk jug (the one we actually had been shooting at earlier) and the BB ricocheted off and came back in his eye. Our parents bought it at the time. Luckily, nothing permanent happened. The BB hit Scott's eyelid. But the next day, with a patch over his eye, Scott had to break the gun in half and throw it away. It was a rule that his father and mother had issued — that if he ever got hurt, the gun would be destroyed. It didn't matter if it was his fault or not.

I was having a lot of trouble socially in junior high school. I was not a fighter, but rather a runner. I had the BEST bowl haircut, big front teeth and a BIG mouth. If someone picked on me, I would find a way to get away from them and/or I would use words, sometimes vulgar words, to fight back. I was never the one to physically fight. I guess I was more afraid of what my mom would do to me if I got in trouble than if I got into a fight. Mom and Dad sought out a therapist for me who was one of my dad's colleagues, "Doc D." as he was referred to by most. Talking with Doc D. was always fun. Each time we met, it was more conversational than anything else. We met once a month for about a year. One Friday afternoon, my mom picked me up from school. As we were driving she told me that Doc D. had died earlier that day. She said that he wasn't feeling well that morning and wanted to take a nap. He had lain down on a couch in his office and didn't wake up. My dad and another work colleague found him. Even though I was 11 years old, this was one of the first times that I remember feeling a sense of shock hearing about death. Partly because I had just talked with Doc D. a week prior, but also because it started to sink that we don't live forever. A couple nights after he died, I was asleep and I had a very vivid dream of Doc D. floating above my bed. He appeared as himself, didn't say anything, but his body was intertwined with flowing robes.

Jill Mason was a very popular girl in our town and she lived just two houses down from us with her parents and her younger brother Tim. Jill was beautiful and tall. It was as if she had everything going for her, especially with a "Phoebe Cates" look and appeal to her. Sorry if that is an obscure reference for you, but Phoebe Cates was many a guy's crush in the early '80s.

Other kids gravitated toward Jill too, including Holly. Jill was an honor student, cheerleader, lacrosse player and band member; she was involved in a lot of activities both in school and out. Her father also played the banjo outside on their porch often. And if I heard him playing, I would go running over just to listen. He loved the audience. He had a very loud singing voice, and you could hear it from a good distance.

When I was 12, I learned that Jill had developed cancer and that she would be going through treatment in Boston. Aplastic anemia is a bone marrow failure. Her treatments didn't take and she died on August 23, 1982 at age 15. It shocked me as much as the death of Doc D did, but it was different because it was weird to try and comprehend how someone so young, someone with so much life in them, could die. A short while after Jill's death, I was outside and saw Mr. Mason playing catch with Tim in the front yard. I wanted to say something to them, but at 12 years old words don't come to you easily. I think even for some adults, it's not easy. My mom gave me a suggestion. I rode over slowly on my bike and stopped out front of their house. I said "Hi" and that I was sorry to hear about Jill. Mr. Mason thanked me and Tim was silent. I sat there for a couple of minutes and then peddled away.

Mr. Mason never sat on the front porch and played his banjo after that, but I did see him outside one day and went over. I asked him if he was going to be playing the banjo and he didn't say much. He was just sitting in deep thought. They moved from that house a few months later.

3

Bud

Scott's father Lewis (everyone called him Bud) was a senior chief when he was in the Navy. When I was a kid and went over to Scott's house, Bud was usually fixing something in the garage, just like my father. Always next to him was an open can of Budweiser, hence the nickname. A long-running family joke was that Bud really liked wearing a pair of camouflage shorts emblazoned with the Budweiser logo across one of the pockets. Scott, his sisters and mom would all poke fun at him, but he wore them proudly.

After high school, I went to a small vocational college in northern Maine to pursue my interest in computers. I had no interest in going to a four-year college at the time, nor was I interested in a specialized degree. At the time, I just wanted to write programs and create video games. Colleges that taught those skills weren't around in the late 1980s. And much to my disappointment, the classes at this school were focused only on writing business-based computer programs.

A year later Scott attended the same school, but went for a business degree. It was great having Scott to pal around with in northern Maine. We had mutual friends, and with us being friends it also helped me to form new connections that I probably would not have made had he not been there. On Saturday nights we usually went to Canada to hit the nightclubs. You only had to be 19 to get into these places, and it was well worth the 90-minute trek. One snowy frigid night in February 1990, a group of us were headed up to Canada. On a back road, Scott was driving up ahead in his car with one of our friends, and I was with another friend, Mike, who was driving a few more of us up in his old Dodge a few miles back. A short while later we came upon an accident. In the middle of the road was an older pickup, sideways and hazard lights flashing. The front end of the pickup had been smashed in. But it was the shock of seeing Scott and his passenger getting out of his car, which had been sent, sideways, 15 feet into a deep snowbank on the side of the road, that got me. The front end of his car — totaled! Grateful that Scott was OK, once the cops cleared the accident and Scott's car was towed away, we all piled into Mike's car and headed over to the house of one of our friends who happened to live nearby. Scott asked to go upstairs to call home and let them know what had happened. I could hear him talking, he was frustrated and angry at himself, and I heard him yell to the person on the phone, "But that was my car!" Then I heard him cry. He collected himself and we carried on into Canada that night. A few weeks later, when I asked him why he had been upset, he said that he had been talking to his dad at the time and when he yelled "But that was my car!", his dad had replied, "But you're my son." Scott walked away with his life, but also knowing how much he meant to his father. It helped that Scott's family was very tight. Whenever there was a difficult family situation, they put away any disagreements they may have had between them and came together as one to work through the situation.

A few months later in May, our college celebrated "Tech Day." This annual event was designed to congratulate the graduating seniors, but truth be told, it was just a party day for the entire student body. We couldn't party on our "dry" campus, and it was not worth getting caught even if you were 21. Instead, the students would congregate a few miles away, down a long dirt road at the Broken Bridge. I drove a group of my other friends down the bridge that morning. I knew from the previous year that this was only round one of two for that day. And by 1 p.m., most of the partygoers were already shitfaced. We headed back to campus so that the others could sleep off this first round before going onto the next round later that night. As I pulled into our parking lot I saw Scott walking slowly with his hands in his pockets. I didn't think much of it, but he hadn't been with us at the Broken Bridge. We were usually together, but with his job, I figured he had to work that day. I rolled down my window and asked him what he was doing. He looked over, saw me and said, "I'll talk to you later." I parked and walked into the apartment we shared.

Our other roommate Ben said, "Did you hear?"

"No..."

"Scott's dad died this morning."

"What?!" My heart sank. How could this be? How? What happened? Ben said something about a heart attack and a boat. I ran out looking for Scott. I went over to the dorm; he wasn't there. I asked around and no one had seen him. I went into a private phone room at the dorm and called my mom and dad. Mom said that Scott's family was looking for him and I told her that I had just seen him.

I was on a mission to find Scott. His family was worried about him and they had no way to contact him directly. Finally I called his work, and he was there. In the only way I knew how to make light of this difficult situation, I tried to crack a joke. It didn't go over well. He was just silent and hung up.

The very next morning we set out on the six-hour road trip back to Brunswick. Scott was in his car ahead of me the whole way. I had so many thoughts and questions flying through my head. What was all of this going to mean? How was this possible? Was there any chance that this was a joke? I knew that at the very least I was headed back to be with my family, but he was headed back into a storm.

When we arrived at his house, Scott got out of his car and somberly walked toward the front door. His sister came out and they embraced and cried. It was as emotional as you could imagine. I hugged both of them and left to go to my home.

These were going to be the first funeral services I would ever attend. I didn't go to the wake because I didn't know what to expect. But on the day of the funeral, when my entire family walked into the funeral home, I was looking for Scott. I was also looking for his dad, but couldn't see anything because our family was ushered into a separate room in this old house that had been converted into a funeral home in Brunswick. There were a lot of people there too. As the funeral service was ending, we were given the opportunity to give our condolences to Scott's family in a receiving line. As we approached them, I caught

Bud's casket out of the corner of my eye and I only looked at him lying there once. It was surreal. It was Bud, but he wasn't animated any longer. He was still. He looked like was peacefully sleeping and you wanted to just go up to shake him and wake him up so that everything would go back to normal.

Bud's family had come in from Indiana, including his father. He sat stoically, looking at his son's casket. As I got to Scott, we just looked at each other. I shook his hand, looked him straight in the eye, and smiled. Later that night at his house, I was able to sit with Scott's mom, Pat, and Bud's father. They were reminiscing about Bud and his father said something that stuck with me for many years: "A man should never bury his child. It ain't right."

After the funeral services in Brunswick, they had Bud's body flown to Memphis, where he received a full military funeral service with a 21-gun salute. Scott picked up the shell casings and put them in the folded flag that was handed to his mother. He then started to walk away from the service before it was done. He didn't know where he was going, he just needed to be away. A family friend, Christy, caught up with him and walked side by side with him, not saying a word. He said that it was the hardest time for him, but he appreciated that someone was walking with him. Later that night, Scott and his sister Cory sat on the bluff of the Mississippi River, while the Memphis in May festival was going on around them. They talked late into the night and drank beer until they were drunk.

In the aftermath of this loss, Scott said that he just kept "busy" to get through it, for what seemed like months. I asked him when things finally slowed down for him, and he told me that things didn't really slow down at all. He just kept going and it's still going to this day. It's life, but "there isn't a day that goes by that I don't think about him," he says.

Just a couple months before his dad died, Scott's parents had planned to move to Memphis, Tennessee. Scott and I had come home for spring break that year and we both saw the 'For Sale' sign out front of his house. It caught us both by surprise. In fact, Scott's momPat had been in Memphis looking for homes and visiting with one of Scott's older sisters, Sharon, the day Bud died. But just one month after Bud's death, their house in Brunswick sold. A couple weeks before they moved, they held a massive yard sale. Pat told me recently that instead of holding onto Bud's stuff permanently, she just grabbed all of his clothes and other things and put them out at the sale that morning. "What good was it going to do to keep it?" It was especially hard for her to let Bud's Budweiser camo shorts go.

It's been 27 years since Bud's death. I asked Scott what were three things he's learned along the way since that time.

1. He learned how to love and to he learned to open up, especially after seeing how heartbroken his mom was about losing Bud.
2. He said that we shouldn't take the life we're given and waste it — life goes on and you do, too.
3. Finally, be a role model for your kids and other kids, rather than a dumbass. "The world has too many dumbasses!" Scott and his wife Sunita now spend their time raising their son Michael Lewis.

31

Early in 2017, I had the opportunity to sit down and talk with retired U.S. Wildland firefighter Rex Mann. Rex reminds me of my father and of Bud — salt of the earth, and wise. Rex and I spoke about death and loss. I was curious to learn about his view of how we are dealing with death in this day and age. He said, "Back in the day [the 1940s], we were much closer to the act of dying. It was more 'earthy.' The body was put into the home and people came to the home to pay their respects. Everyone came and saw that, they were part of the process of death. There was a time in our country's history when life had to go on — care for the kids, cook dinner, take care of the home, etc. We live in a world now where people don't 'die' anymore, they pass away."

Rex went on and offered some sage advice: "We have to grieve, for sure. But we can't just sit in a corner and sulk. Go get busy doing something to get unstuck. It's not forgetting the person that died, it's *honoring them that you're carrying on.* There is some point when dwelling [on the loss] is destructive of your true purpose."

In a November 29, 2014 blog post on *The Huffington Post* titled "Death, Passed Away, or Passed," author William B. Bradshaw sought to ask the very question of why we have moved from the term "dead" to "passed away" or "passed." William recalls going to a funeral where the minister referred to the man having "died," but the obituary referred to the man having "passed away." William went on to interview several funeral directors about when this changed, and while none of them could recall a specific time, in today's world they too refer to death as "passing away." And for the most part it's been like this for 25 years. One director said, "It just seemed to evolve."

Another point taken from every funeral director interviewed was that "...the use of 'passed away' seems more gentle, not so harsh, and less cold than 'died.'" This was an indication of the genuine concern that all the funeral directors expressed for the healing and comfort of the families of the deceased. One funeral director suggested that the use of 'passed away' instead of 'died' is also an indication of "...the times we live in — an era when people in general tend to prolong facing up to the hard facts of difficult situations as long as possible."

Rex Mann addressed this too. "We're being politically correct even with death." I couldn't agree more! If this trend continues, pretty soon life will be referred to as breathing carefully! It seems that since the terms 'death' and 'died' shifted to 'passed away,' we have not been living in *our nature* to deal with mortality as our ancestors dealt with it. The seasons of our life match that of the world we live in. As my mentor Bo Eason would say, "If we go against Mother Nature, we lose." New growth emerges every spring. Life goes on — look around you.

William goes on to ask, "Why then, did the minister use the term 'died'? In the Christian faith, and even in the modern Bible, the terms die and death are used, not 'passed away.'" He concludes his article by saying, "...I would find it difficult to use 'passed away' or 'passed.' Neither of these implies a complete and absolute finality or death to this way of living. I believe that we must die in order to live..."

4

Albert Thompson

One day when Anna was 14, some girls were making fun of her at school and said to her, "You must be a daddy's girl."

Nonchalantly she replied, "No, he died of some disease." Silence...

When she thought about that interaction with the girls further, it occurred to her that she really didn't know how her father, Albert, had died when she was 5 years old. She asked her mom about this, and her mother said, "Why don't we talk about it at another time." But Anna wanted to know. She felt she needed to know.

A few months later, Anna was at her cousin's house for a birthday party. They were up in her cousin's bedroom when Anna was compelled to ask her cousin if she knew how her father died. "Yes, but I can't tell you…" Seething, Anna thought to herself, "You know how my father died, but you're not going to tell me?!" Full of anger and pain, she started crying heavily. Her aunt came in to the bedroom and she knew right away why Anna was crying. She suggested that Anna stay over for the weekend to talk about it, but Anna demanded to know right then and there. Taking a deep breath, her aunt told her, "He took his life in the basement of a bakery he was working in." Stunned, Anna felt like her whole life had been changed in an instant. Some bits and pieces of what she had heard over the years began to unfold and make sense. Something about Albert hurting a little boy when he was 11, but she didn't know if any of that information was true. So she asked her aunt about the little boy, but her aunt didn't want to tell her directly.

Instead, the next day they went to the library to sort through many films of microfiche, to locate an 11-page article that was written in a magazine in 1986. The article was overwhelming for Anna as she read about an 11-year-old Albert killing a 6-year-old boy while they were playing in the woods behind Albert's house. She was also struggling to resolve the loss of her father as a suicide, which she had just learned about the day before. The emptiness and anger from not having her father around while she was growing up welled up. She said that her memories of her father were only good ones.

Just recently, Anna heard her father's voice again on some old cassette recordings that were found in her grandmother's house. These recordings were done by the man and woman who had interviewed Albert for that particular magazine article. Anna had completely forgotten what her father sounded like. But she said his voice was very polite and gentle. On the tapes, he owned everything that happened when he was a young boy. He remembered physical and sexual abuse at the hands of his stepfather, but he didn't remember taking the younger boy's life.

Later in the recordings, the interviewers asked Albert why his mom hadn't done more to protect him and his brother. Albert told them that he had absolved his mom of any wrongdoing long ago because she too was abused by the stepfather. She was a divorced woman with two boys and she was doing the best that she could do at the time. This was back before women could get a decent-paying job to support kids as a single parent — we're talking the early 1970s.

Anna told me that as the recording went on, the woman interviewer asked some fairly intense questions — she challenged everything Albert said. She asked, "Why did you go back to your hometown? Why would you want to back to where it happened? Why would you want to do that and look people in the eye...you worked as the head of the housing authority, the place where you killed a little boy. Why would you go back there?"

Calmly Albert replied, "...Ma'am, at 11 years old I was taken from my home. To me, no matter where you are in life, you ALWAYS want to go back home. And I felt like this was home to me. And the people who hated me, wanted me gone, were small in comparison to the people that were compassionate towards me..." Hearing her father's voice was a tremendous gift for Anna. She had forgotten what it sounded like. It was something that she will always cherish, and also misses every day.

Anna's perspective of her father is that Albert had tried hard to help others so that he would in some way make up for what had happened when he was a young boy. But there wasn't a day that went by when he didn't punish himself for the life he took. He was looking for redemption and forgiveness that never came.

Anna was told that her father had not wanted to do the interview, but the magazine told him that they would be publishing an article regardless of whether he talked. So he sought to have the magazine be the voice of reason and mercy for him. However, it did not serve as any type of redemption or mercy for Albert at all, but rather reopened many of the wounds for everyone involved. The mother of the little boy died shortly after the article came out and ultimately, the weight was too much for Albert, who took his life a few months later.

Anna has had two decades to process not only how her father died, but also what led him to take his life. She works hard to focus on the good in people, on being a good parent to her son, and to live life to its fullest.

5

A baby!

When I was 27 years old, I became an instant dad to a 2-year-old girl, Arminda and an 8-year-old boy, Christos. My girlfriend Maria was six months pregnant with her third child, who was mine. And while we all thought the baby was going to be a boy, the ultrasounds were showing that there was an 85 percent chance I didn't put the nuts on the bolt.

Maria and I were up in Maine over a long summer weekend to visit my parents and one day while we were there, we chose to grab lunch on the patio of the Lobster Cooker restaurant in Freeport. It was a really beautiful sunny day, 75 degrees. It was the perfect time to resume an earlier discussion that we had about baby names. Holding her Greek traditions sacred, Maria wanted to name the baby after my mother. My mom's name is Kristina, and there were already five people named "Kris," "Chris" or some other variation of "Chris" inside the immediate family, so that was out.

We started to explore names that were outside of the traditional naming, and what was best representative of the newly forming family dynamic. I didn't know much Greek at the time, still don't actually, so I asked Maria what the Greek word was for "freedom." That's *Elefthereea*. I asked what the Greek word for "hope" was; that is *Elpeetha*. And then I asked what the Greek word for "life" was, and that is *Zoi*. I loved how that name sounded and how it was spelled. I especially loved that it was nontraditional.

On October 18, 1998 at 5:10 p.m., Zoi Kristina Hodgdon was born. While the doctor and nurses were tending to Maria, there laying in this plexiglass cradle was this baby girl, with my nose, and few other noticeable features of her mom and me. But I was really scared that I was now 100 percent responsible for this child. I sat down and I folded my arms along the edge of the cradle and stared at this baby who was trying to open her new eyes. I looked at her and quietly said, "I love you and I want you to know that I am going to do everything in my power to be the best dad for you."

6

Six of one, half dozen of the other

Zoi's first six years were a balancing act. Not only for all of us in this new family dynamic of a new marriage — three kids and a mother-in-law living with us — but also with Zoi's health. At age 3, she contracted shingles. This eventually progressed into full-blown childhood Graves' disease. Ultimately, Zoi had to have her thyroid out at age 5, thus putting her on a medication that she would have to take for the rest of her life.

When Zoi's mom and I broke up in 2005, it was one of the hardest things that all three kids had to deal with. Divorce just sucks! It's a huge loss for the family and each person in the family. And the kids have no input as to what happens. They go along with a 'new normal.' At that time Zoi was 6, Arminda was 10 and Christos was 16. I felt especially bad about the situation because the familiar family dynamic was changing permanently and there was nothing I could do to fix it, other than to be there for the kids like a dad should be. I chose to stay in the local area to be close to them.

After the divorce was finalized, the routine of visitations took place and we all tried to carry on as best as possible given the new family dynamic. The next six years proved to be an ongoing adjustment for us all. Some things worked great, but then some things did not. Ultimately, I had to make a decision to fight for custody of Zoi.

7

Beaches

One weekend in late September 2012, I asked Zoi if she wanted to go to Duxbury Beach here in Massachusetts. It is a location that always brings great memories for me and the girls. When they were growing up it was a place we frequented often. We went there mostly in the summertime, but we also went sometimes in the winter when no one else was there. Duxbury Beach is a very long beach, but not very wide: at high tide there are about 30 feet between the marsh grass and the water. At low tide, the water goes out pretty far. No matter where you are on the beach there are a ton of rocks, some of which we would collect and bring back to the house. I probably have a few hundred rocks in the house from our beach excursions back then.

By 2012 I hadn't taken the girls there for a couple of years, though. And, since there had been a lot of family-related stressors hitting all of us, when the opportunity presented itself, I grabbed Zoi and went that day. When we arrived, she walked around like she was being refreshed by the sounds of the waves crashing against the shore and just being there. She let her feet soak in the cold sea spray, and then we just walked for a while. Waves crashing, no one really around us, I could see that she was deep in thought. And, like the ocean had done for us in the past, I was hoping that this would help clear her head. The best part was that this was a solid two hours of time together with her.

As we pulled out of the beach parking lot, I asked Zoi if we would ever be living on the beach. She replied "Yes!" very quickly. I asked when — giving her the opportunity to offer her vision of the future that didn't yet exist. She went into intricate detail and told me the age I would be, and where the house would be located, as well as the color and style of the house itself. I asked if I was together with anyone, and she said "yes" — a woman who moved there recently to begin her life over again too. Zoi and I talked at length about this future home and I could see it was helping her clear her head even more as she focused on that vision.

A few days later, I posed the same questions to Arminda. The details she gave me were almost identical to those of Zoi. It was a very powerful connection to say the least, and it was great to connect with both girls on that level.

8

Two Christmases

A couple months had passed since I took Zoi to the beach. We were coming off a particularly difficult set of months for both of the girls actually, and it was just nice to have them home on Christmas day. We spent Christmas Eve at their aunt and uncle's house with all of their cousins and extended family. All of the girls were wearing matching PJs and we all laughed a lot that night. We drove home late in a light snow. Christmas morning we woke up and the three of us opened our gifts. I had previously bought Zoi an electronic drum set and the two girls were up in their shared bedroom laughing and putting together the drums. My phone rang and it was their uncle. I said "Merry Christmas! It was great seeing you last night." He replied, "There was an accident overnight and their cousin Christos didn't make it." My heart sank. You can't be serious, I thought. Not this, not now! I didn't know what to say to my brother-in-law, except that I was so very sorry. He acknowledged and said that we'd be hearing from Maria shortly, and hung up.

With the girls still laughing upstairs and knowing everything was going to change in an instant, I felt completely helpless. I went to the basement and tried to call my therapist, Zoi's therapist, anyone that I could to help me with this. I did hear from both therapists, yet I felt no comfort as they told me the same thing. I had to tell the girls. My heart was beating out of my chest when I walked upstairs. Still hearing laughter as I walked into their room, I told them I had some very difficult news to share with them.

One year later, after being hospitalized on a few occasions, and now living in a therapeutic home for adolescents, Zoi was able to come home to my house for a couple of days over that Christmas.

We woke up Christmas morning and it was sunny. I think in some way we were all expecting the phone to ring like it had one year prior. But thankfully it didn't. The girls and I opened Christmas gifts. Zoi painted me an amazingly peaceful picture of a Buddha sleeping. The girls were excited about their gifts and later that morning, we spent time at my sister's house. It was good to see my girls hanging out with their cousins like they had on previous Christmases. There were a lot of laughs between them.

Earlier in December, I had been contemplating taking the girls to a Prince concert as one of their surprise Christmas gifts. I wanted to start creating new memories for all of us on this first anniversary of their cousin's death. Creating new memories creates light in what could otherwise be a very dark time in your life. When we experience loss, any loss, anniversaries and holidays are always hard. They can amplify

45

the feeling of that loss. But these days may also provide the opportunity to amplify the feelings of happiness, so why not go out and do something for yourself that creates a new memory around that anniversary date?

The girls knew many of Prince's songs because I was always playing his music in the car. They especially liked "Alphabet St." and "Starfish and Coffee." When I thought about this opportunity more, I realized it had been 16 years since I had last seen Prince in concert and I didn't know if I would get another opportunity like this. No more justification needed; I scooped the tickets up. The timing of the concert was perfect, too. It was a Friday night and I would have been picking up Zoi for the weekend anyway. I didn't tell the girls about this gift until the day of the concert.

Arminda had been at my house the morning of the concert and I asked her, if she could see anyone in concert, who would it be? She said, without hesitation, Prince. I just smiled and said "Well guess who we are seeing tonight?" She screamed. It was beautiful. We then called Zoi and I asked her the same thing: "If you could see anyone in concert, who would it be?" "Um, Prince." "Well, guess where we are going tonight?" She screamed, and then Arminda screamed and it was beautiful.

I picked up Zoi and we all drove down to Mohegan Sun Casino listening to Prince the entire way. It was freezing that night. When we entered the arena, our seats were directly above the right side of the stage. It was a great view.

Esperanza Spaulding opened for Prince. It was good music and Zoi was getting into it. When that set finished, the lights went out. The place went nuts! Both Zoi and Arminda were very excited and couldn't wait. The opening song was "Days of Wild" and then Prince went right into "1999." Two and a half hours later, all three of us were still dancing and singing, and after one encore, Prince's band came back out for a second. When I heard the opening riff of "Purple Rain" I looked over at Zoi as she clenched her fists in victory. It was an epic rendition, and the video of that performance is still available on YouTube.

Sharing this with the girls was so very special for me and them. We were heading in a new and different direction and it was awesome. We left there exhausted, but happy.

9

Jonathan Frusciante's guitar

A month later, in late January 2014, I had been doing my usual weekend tasks — cleaning the house, working on my Beachbody coaching business and getting tax paperwork together. I went to pick up Zoi and knocked on her mother's front door. Zoi came out in a red fleece jacket that I had gotten for her a couple years prior, black jeans and her combat boots. Her style was pretty rad. I had forgotten that she even had the red jacket. Her colored hair was pulled back in a bun. I glanced over at her as we walked down the stairs. I asked her how she was and she muttered "good." We got into the car and she asked to go to the local Indian Bazaar store to get some incense and to look around. I had never been into that store before and agreed to go in with her. When we walked inside she brought me to the aisle where all the incense was. It smelled great. She picked up two different kinds that were her favorites, rose petal and jasmine. At the checkout counter she spotted a little figurine of an elephant. In Buddhism, elephants are symbols of mental strength, earthiness and responsibility. She asked for one of the figurines, along with a tube of henna ink. She paid for everything with cash and we headed home.

We pulled into my driveway and went inside. Zoi greeted our dog Bean and went right up to her room to do her "teen" things. Earlier in the day I had purchased Zoi's favorite movie, Fight Club, but didn't tell her about it yet. I hadn't seen the movie before and wanted to surprise her and watch it with her over the weekend.

I went upstairs to see what was up like I always did. She had changed into a different outfit. Music was playing in the background, the jasmine incense was lit, a string of Christmas lights was lit around the perimeter of her room, and she was applying the henna ink, which had the most acrid smell to it. She was making a really cool sun design too. I went downstairs to work on my tax paperwork and she came down. I asked if she wanted to hang out with any of her friends, and she said no. I asked if she wanted to watch a movie, and she said no. I didn't tell her it was Fight Club just yet. She went back upstairs to change into yet another outfit. I cleaned up my paperwork and went upstairs to see if she wanted to make some kale chips — she happily said "Yes!"

After we cleaned up, she said she was tired and wanted to go to bed. She gave me a very long and strong hug. "I love you, Pumpkins." "I love you too, dad." She went back upstairs. I went back to my computer for a little bit before going up to check on her before I went

49

to bed.

When I opened her door again, I could hear Jonathan Frusciante's guitar playing softly on her stereo, the only lights on in the room were that same string of Christmas lights around the perimeter, but she wasn't in her bed. In the dim light and out of the corner of my eye, I could see that she was standing in her closet and I thought she was going to jump out and scare me. I was going to call her bluff and said, "Zoi, what are you doing?"

She didn't answer me.

She wasn't standing in her closet.

I called 911.

It was so cold and windy that night. I was in the passenger seat of a Norwood police car as we raced toward town at speeds of over 60 MPH. The volume on the officer's CB radio was practically muted, yet I could hear several clicks of transmissions ending. He didn't want me to hear something. All of the buildings and streetlights were going by in a blur. And in between my repeated "Holy shit!" statements of disbelief, I must have asked the officer five times in the two-mile trip to the hospital "Is she breathing?!" Each time his reply was "I don't know..." and he accelerated more.

10

This is not real

"Call time, 11:25 p.m.," the ER doctor called out. I thought, this is not real. So many people in that room. All looking at me like they knew this was going to suck. Her mom was crying so hard that no sound was coming out while she was screaming for them to not stop working on her. This is not real. The police wanted to talk to me fairly soon afterward. They told me they were sorry for my loss. I started making phone calls to my family and friends around midnight in between the repeated "Holy shit!"'s that I was saying to myself as I paced the halls of the hospital. I don't even remember who I called first. This is not real.

Zoi's aunt and uncle (Maria's brother) showed up first. I called my sister and she raced over. I didn't want to call my mom and dad, but had to. That sucked. I called Scott and my therapist. Christos and his friend were at the hospital with Maria. All of us stunned and numb. I didn't know what to do about Arminda as my heart sank even deeper trying to figure out how to break this news to her. I just kept thinking that this could not be real.

A couple hours later, the hospital staff said that we could stay as long as we wanted to with Zoi, but I didn't want to remember her like this. I said goodbye like she was sleeping, I kissed her forehead and told her that I'd see her again soon. My sister drove me back to my house and I didn't sleep.

PART II

A DEEP BREATH

"Everything that has a beginning, has an ending. Make
your peace with that and all will be well."
— The Buddha

11

The morning sun

It was a beautiful sunny day that Sunday morning. Crisp and cool, the kind of morning when I would normally make bacon and eggs for Zoi and Arminda. I had a searing pain in my gut and I wasn't hungry in the least.

Having to tell people that you lost your child, less than 12 hours afterward…is just, well, both surreal and the absolute worst feeling, ever. I'm not going to lie, you *don't* want to do it, nobody does. It doesn't even seem possible that you *could* be saying something like that to anyone. It didn't feel real.

I reached out to Anna:

"Hey can I call you back, is everything OK?"

"No…"

"OK, I'll call you in a…. wait, what?"

"We lost Zoi last night."

She just broke down crying and raced over. When Anna came into my house, she was stunned too. She just looked at me and my sister in disbelief. She later told me that she had many thoughts about her own relation to this same type of loss with her father swirling around in her mind as she tried to make some sense of this too. She had known somewhat about the custody battle going on, but she also knew Zoi from styling and coloring her hair.

Shock turned to worry for me as to how Arminda would be hearing the news. It was so hard to even think that this was going to be said to her, let alone anyone else. Later that Sunday morning my house started to fill up with my family and friends. All of us were there to begin this new journey without Zoi here with us. My nieces arrived that afternoon, and my heart sank. My mom and dad came in and it was the same thing over and over — hugging and crying. Scott arrived at my house that afternoon. A lot of hugging and crying. Arminda arrived at the house carrying one of Zoi's blankets and a Christmas picture from when Zoi was much younger. She had just come from Maria's house. I ran outside and met her in the driveway. We just embraced and cried for a while. All that I could tell her was that I was so very sorry. Immediately, I got a jolt of pain and I wanted it to stop. I didn't want any of us to be here, especially like this. There didn't seem to be a way out, though, only a way through it. The house was full and I was completely exhausted. That evening, I went into my living room and sat down on my couch. My mom was on the phone with a friend. I put my head down and the best thing that could have happened, did. Bean got up and planted herself next to me. There we both slept all night.

The next morning, Arminda wanted to go over to Maria's house again, and I felt compelled to go too. When we went in, Arminda hugged Maria. Then Maria and I embraced for the first time in nine years. She started to rattle off dates in between the sobs — January 21, 1998 (the day Zoi was conceived). October 18th (Zoi's birthday). It was so hard to see her like this. But we had other plans to make now.

12

A deep breath and the week of preparing

Monday morning I woke up and knew I had to let the rest of the world, my world, know about Zoi's death. While it wasn't traditional, I posted one of my favorite pictures of Zoi and shared the following on Facebook:

Sorrow and peace fill me now. My daughter Zoi has passed away. She left our world late Saturday night and will be greatly missed by everyone that even knew her name. A powerful spirit who loved unconditionally and gave unselfishly, Zoi struggled for a period of time. She was at peace with herself in the end.

Please send prayers and love and SMILE when you think of Zoi. That's how she would want to be remembered. It will be OK, I know it will be.

My phone started to ring off the hook with some of my old friends from Brunswick reaching out. Pretty soon, her close friends began to show up. By the end of the day, the house was filled with many of the kids whom Zoi shared her life with. Jerry, Neto, Amanda all came over and stayed the entire week. It felt so good for all of us amidst this pain. They were all looking to me to see if this was real. They were *all* just looking for something that could help them to understand, why Zoi? I was grateful to be connected to them then, as they all collectively reminded me of her. I didn't care that any or all of them were there too. It just felt right. And in truth, it felt like Zoi was there with us in so many ways. It was not hearing her laugh or voice that kept throwing me off.

The entire week I was hoping against all hope that I would get a call from the hospital that Zoi had miraculously come back to life. I wanted that so badly. But the call never came, of course. The house remained full with all of her friends and cousins who slept over. It was comforting for us to be together. We laughed, we cried, we watched movies, we even took a giant goofball selfie with everyone in the house.

We also pressed on with preparing for Zoi's wake and funeral services. Maria and I picked out her clothes. The high-waisted pants, a white top, her combat boots, a red fleece jacket and black-and-white–striped beanie. Arminda and I sat in our kitchen with the funeral director and chose a casket. We were laughing that Zoi would be pissed if we got her a pink one. Despite any laughs though, all of this had to be done, and I hated every second of it. Christos and I went over to the cemetery to look at the spot where Zoi would be buried. It was the first spot in that row and it was hard to visualize anything other than the grass beneath our feet at the time.

It felt like I was being pulled into a vortex that I had zero possibility of getting out of. I did, however, know that with my family and friends around, this *was* possible to navigate. Sometimes, it felt like getting to the next minute was all we could focus on. Maybe it was even the next hour, or even the next day. One thing remained true — life goes on.

13

A deep breath and the wake

It was sunny the day of the wake. I spent the day feeling both unprepared for what lay ahead, but also strangely comforted that I'd be seeing Zoi again. Early in the afternoon I remembered the two necklaces. As our relationship was forming, Maria and I had necklaces that were symbolic of our strong connection. Mine was of smiling sunshine, hers was three beads — a daisy, rose and daisy design. We had worn these for the first few years of our relationship, and never took them off. As the strings wore out, we replaced them a couple of times. Ultimately, we decided to make them a permanent part of us: in 2002, we got the images tattooed on us. The plan was that these necklaces were supposed to be handed over to Zoi when she got older. It was more than fitting that she received them now for her new journey.

I went searching for the necklaces in my attic crawlspace. When I opened the box I had thought they were in, they weren't there! I looked in a couple other boxes, and when I couldn't locate them I got really pissed at myself. "Where the fuck are these things?!" "I hate when I do that! I always put shit some place where I'm supposed to remember where it was, but it's not there!" This was not the day to lose anything. But, I really don't lose stuff often…I just couldn't think straight that week even if I tried. I looked for over an hour. My friends James and Leslie were with me, asking me if the necklaces were possibly in another location in the house. All they could do was stay with me. They both were just trying to calm me so that I could focus and look for them. Sobbing, my eyes unclear, I pulled box after box out from the crawlspace. I grew increasingly more frustrated and scared that I wouldn't find them. I pulled out the very last box, tucked way in the back. It was the box of Zoi's baby clothes. Inside also contained a blue small square box. As I opened that little box, the two necklaces spilled out in my hand. I felt so much relief in finding them.

It was time to go over to the funeral home and I had no idea what was going to happen when we got there. The funeral home was at the end of the street where Maria and I used to live, and where Zoi grew up. When we arrived my heart was beating out of my chest. Arminda had not seen Zoi since right before she went back to college for her second semester as a freshman. Arminda and I walked in together first. We peered through the doorway, and at the end of this rather long room was Zoi. I saw her black-and-white–striped beanie and her red coat. As we approached her, Arminda was shaking. This was so hard. I remember telling Arminda that what we were seeing now was just the vessel for Zoi's soul and that it did what it was supposed to do for her, and that her soul was somewhere else now. It may have comforted me, but not so much Arminda in this moment.

Dad and Mom stepped up. Dad had brought along the aviator wings he earned when he became a pilot in the Navy. He pinned them on the lapel of Zoi's coat. He told her that she had earned her wings.

Maria arrived a short while later. I went out to her and together we walked into the room. It was so hard seeing the mother of my child cry over our daughter. This was all so very surreal and I wished it wasn't happening, none of it. I wanted to just turn back the clock so very much. Maria's sisters came over to her and helped her to a seat on the side of the room.

As more relatives came in it was feeling more and more like Zoi was there with us, but in a different form. Her energy was there and I could feel it. I wasn't sad at all during the wake. I just felt like I needed to be her dad and everyone else's dad that day, to care for each and every person who came through to pay their respects to her and our family. The number of people who came to Zoi's wake was unreal. Over 900. Relatives, Zoi's friends, people that knew the family, people that didn't know the family, my friends, colleagues, people in and around town. The line never stopped. So many of Zoi's friends and schoolmates were coming through — very upset. Some of them were peeking around others ahead of them to see Zoi. Every one of them who came up, I gave a huge hug to and said that it was going to be OK. That Zoi would want them to remember all of the good times that they had together. As more and more people came up to share stories of Zoi with me and to tell me how much Zoi inspired them, impacted them and gave them hope, and to tell me that they were sorry for my loss, I was sorry for THEIR loss because I knew what we were all going to be missing. Her energy, her smile, her mad ukulele skills, her free spirit nature, her voice...and most of all, her philosophy of life to "just be."

The wake was from 4 to 8 p.m., but the line was still going strong at 8:30. By 9 we had to stop. If they had allowed another five hours, I would have stayed there as long as I needed to. Nine hundred people. Wow. It still amazes me that she touched *that* many lives. I am forever grateful for them for coming.

14

A deep breath and the funeral

The next day at the funeral I don't remember a single word that the Greek priests said to me or my family during the service. I don't even remember who was in the church. I sat feet away from Zoi and kept wondering what was next for all of us. I envisioned this mess being a pile of string that had various colors, knots in some areas, all intertwined and tangled. The end of the string was sticking out from the bottom of this pile about three inches. That little bit of the string was this funeral service and the pile was what lay ahead of us.

I talk about this analogy because when it comes to the struggles in our life, we tend to want to tackle the entire pile of string at once. But we know we can't tackle our struggles that way. We need a way to pull only some of the string out as move through the struggle, and at the same time untangle the knots as we come to them. What we have at the other end of the pile is not a pile at all, but rather a combed-out, guided walk through our grief.

At the end of the service, I was asked to come up to say final words to Zoi. As I approached her, I broke down. This was the last time that I would be seeing her — forever. And like I did when she was born, standing over the plexiglass cradle the day she born, I stood over her silver casket and said, "Always and forever Zoi, I love you." I placed a few items in with her: a journeying Buddha figurine from her bedroom, an open box of jasmine incense, her paintbrushes, and finally a flutter of kisses on her forehead like I had always given her since she was a baby. Her mom brought up a figurine of a woman carrying her heart and she put that in with her. The priests said a few prayers in Greek that I have yet to remember, and covered her face with a white cloth. The one sound I remember is the audible click of the casket lid being closed.

Damn it.

The Massachusetts State Police provided an escort over to the cemetery, for which I am grateful. When we arrived at her resting place, everyone had gathered around. Maria, Christos, Arminda and I were seated a few feet away from the casket while the priest said some additional words that I have yet to remember. Imagine sitting a few feet from a silver casket, white flowers beautifully covering the silver top, 50 degrees outside on the first of February, not a cloud in the sky, and 50 or so loved ones standing by in complete silence. The only sound was of the light wind blowing past our ears.

Afterward, we made our way over to the reception. When we

walked in, there was a sign that read "Zoi Upstairs" and I thought to myself, Yes, yes she is. The reception was mostly family and some close friends. Oddly, I kept looking around for Zoi and had to catch myself on several occasions when I didn't see her.

Damn it.

Christos and Arminda gave the most beautiful, heartfelt dedications to her. I also tried to say a few words, but the only thing I could think of was mostly that it was going to be OK and that I thanked everyone for coming and supporting us and for loving Zoi. Later, a few of Zoi's friends came in. I didn't have the wherewithal to ask them to come to the reception in the first place, but it meant the world to me that they showed up to support her. It made me feel like Zoi was there with us.

The next day was going to be a completely new day in so many ways, a new life for all of us. It was scary as hell to think about what we were going to do and where we would be going, as if we were running headlong into a dark storm with no end in sight. A deep breath...

15

A very deep breath and so many questions

The week after Zoi was buried, the house began to empty out and my family and friends trickled back to their own lives. For someone who likes a lot of 'alone time' to feel centered, I felt very connected and grateful having everyone at my home for those couple of weeks. It was oddly difficult to have the house to myself again. Many sympathy cards came in the mail. Some I read right away, others a little while later. The love and support I received was just as overwhelming as the silence. I liked going up to Zoi's room, sometimes two and three times a day. The lingering jasmine scent from the many sticks of incense she burned was still present, but I wondered if and when that would dissipate. I remember going to the grocery store for several boxes of tissues and laughing later about color-coordinating the boxes for the rooms I'd be spending most of my time in — the living room, the den, and most important, Zoi's room.

Collecting Zoi's belongings from the therapeutic home was tough. I went there half expecting to see her come to the back door to let me in like she always did. It was so hard walking through the rooms again and not seeing her there. The counselors led me upstairs and into her bedroom. Her side of the room was decorated with Nirvana posters and her artwork, and her bed was neatly made. I didn't want to disturb the room as it was, but had to. I put everything in bags and it hurt because I could still smell her. I brought everything back to my house, including the doodles she drew and saved in one of her dresser drawers. To me, every item, even as small as a worn-out pencil, would remind me of her in some way. A few weeks later, I went back to the therapeutic home to visit. All of her housemates and counselors had signed a written card that had Zoi's picture on it and had attached a bunch of balloons to it. We all stood outside and they let me release them. We watched as the balloons floated way up and out of sight. Everyone was silent. My heart hurt as I'm sure everyone else's did too.

As the grieving started to set in, my mornings consisted of crying as soon as I woke up. Sometimes it lasted a few minutes, other times an hour or more. I was asking the universe for Zoi's return, or at least to provide a connection to her so we could communicate in some way. I wasn't sure about what was next in my life, and my thinking wasn't clear. I felt like I was in a fog. I had no desire to do anything or go anywhere and I wasn't doing any exercise or eating well. I wasn't sleeping well either, for obvious reasons. I did have some moments throughout the days that were better than others though, and that was a good break from the sadness.

For my family and Zoi's friends, I started to have conversations with them about Zoi. It felt good for all of us to connect even more, especially in this early stage of grieving. I focused on asking how they were doing. I focused on how they were processing this. I focused on how we were connecting. Knowing you can provide support — and have it at the same time — is a powerful tool for healing. It's important to connect deeply with others when you are grieving. When we take care of others, it provides a purpose to keep going in the darkest of days. And by looking out for others, it's reciprocated on a visceral level. I certainly felt loved and cared for.

What also became clear early on in the grieving process was that all of our family and friends needed to be guided through this chasm of unknowns, fog and darkness. All of the people impacted by Zoi's death had their own chasm to cross as well. At the base of all of this sadness and grief, one thing stood out to me — death may have taken Zoi's life, but it didn't have to take ours. I knew how much Zoi meant to us, and I especially knew that we were going to get through this together. Arminda was my main focus. I was so upset that she didn't have her partner in crime any longer. It broke my heart and I felt extremely guilty that I didn't save Zoi.

My overall thought was that we had no other choice but to be strong, to take each step and carry on — for ourselves, if not for Zoi. Figuratively, I could see a faint light on the other side of the chasm. It became my mission to fight for myself, my family and all of Zoi's friends, to find that pathway back to better days and that "light." And if they couldn't see that light, then it was up to me to help them at least put one foot in front of the other, with the hope that they would eventually see it too.

Inside of the grieving process, we ask a lot of questions. Some of these questions come to us immediately after our loss. Some come later down the path. For me, each time I asked a new question, it hit me as a new problem to solve. Here's the thing: we often avoid answering the tough questions because in our pain, the last thing we want to do is feel more pain. And these questions are painful to explore and answer. When we don't answer them, however, it keeps us in a survival mode. But a survival mode is supposed to be temporary.

In August of 2017, I conducted a poll online in a grief and loss group:

Knowing there is no timeline for our grief process, if you were to assess where you are right now, would you say: (Please select the one that best represents your current place on this journey)

- I just started to grieve a loss.
- I'm well into my grieving process.
- I am stuck in grief.
- I am surviving and having some better days.
- I am thriving in life again.

The results were staggering: only 13 percent were thriving in life again. And 24 percent were starting, well into, or stuck in their grief.

But 63 percent of the people polled said they were just surviving.

- ○ I am surviving and having some better days
- ● I am thriving in life again
- ○ I am stuck in grief
- ○ I just started to grieve a loss
- ○ I'm well into my grieving process

We are meant to live our lives, not to stay in grief or a full-time survival-mode. As complex humans, when grief enters our life, it hits us pretty hard and we seek meaning, and thus ask questions. For some though, there is an ever-present sense of being stuck in struggle and survival. It doesn't have to be that way. So what are we supposed to do?

What I didn't know at the beginning of my grieving process was how I was going to answer my questions, but what I did know is that I had to start somewhere. When each of these questions is answered by us and us alone, it is a tool we need for our journey to keep moving, to help navigate and cross that chasm, and especially to get out of survival mode. We cannot look outside of ourselves for the answers. We have to look inside. It's hard work, and if it seems too daunting, I would recommend seeking out a therapist, counselor or mentor to help along your journey of answering your questions.

I asked questions like:

- How will I navigate the many firsts — holidays and

anniversaries?

- How are others doing?
- What is my purpose now?
- What's next in my life?
- How am I ever going to move on from this?
- How am I going to get back to my work?
- Are they OK now?
- Did I do enough?
- If I have a friend who is struggling, how can I help?
- Will I ever feel better?
- What if family and friends tell me I should just "get over it already"?
- Why am I here and they are not?
- What if I don't want to be in grief?

In the coming chapters, I'm going to show you a process for answering your questions. Please keep in mind that your journey through grief is, or will be, different than mine. But if we empower ourselves to work through the struggle, our ability to walk through our grief will be a little easier and you will feel ever supported by your own strength.

16

A map for your journey

Navigating grief is one of the hardest things that we will ever have to do in our lifetime. But I've found a way to help along the journey, to use when we need it most. Here is an easy-to-follow process I call MAPS. I've used this process for every question I've asked of myself.

1. Be **MINDFUL** of where you are in your struggles. It's OK to be feeling what you're feeling and when you're feeling it in the present moment. Allowing ourselves to both work through and resolve our grief is so very important, and it's on NO timeline but your own.

2. **APPROACH** each question or struggle openly and look at

both sides. Seeing the question from the other person's perspective is powerful. You have already weathered the storms that have come your way and you are strong enough to weather this one too.

3. **PREDICT** the outcome when the question is answered. In other words, what do you envision your world will look like when the question is answered? How do you feel when the struggle is resolved?

4. Embrace the **SUCK**. It may be a bit harder before it gets easier, and walking through this process will be difficult. But I promise, if you do this, it will be worth it! It's OK and it will be OK. Better days are ahead.

Let's start to explore some of the questions in detail and by using the MAPS process. And remember, you matter, you have support and you're not alone! If at any time this feels like it's going to be too much, then go slow, start with one question and work through it. It's OK, go at your own pace. And if need be, seek out the counsel of a professional.

17

How will I get through the holidays and anniversaries?

The first holiday that we came up on was Valentine's Day. It was just two weeks after we laid Zoi to rest. I thought about how weird it was to be approaching a holiday without Zoi when she'd been alive just a couple weeks before. I knew I'd have my morning crying ritual in place, but I wanted to do something different on that day. I wanted to introduce a positive disruptor that would help me to create a new memory. So instead of just staying in bed with the shades drawn,

I'd get my feet on the floor immediately and go do something. I went to dinner with Arminda and we just reminisced about Zoi. It was so very hard for both of us, especially for her. I felt so much pain for Arminda. Getting out got us out of our heads, though. Turns out this is how I approached each of the holidays and anniversaries that year — by asking, what new memories can we create on these days, despite the fact that it was going to hurt with Zoi not being there? If I thought about asking Zoi directly — would she want me to be unhappy or to be happy? — the conclusion was to go and do something fun, because Zoi would want us to be happy. For her friends, this seemed to help them greatly. Some of them reported back that they went and took photos, or hung out with other friends. They felt supported and cared for too.

Easter was spent with my family up in Maine. It was how I chose to work through this holiday. This was one of Zoi's favorite holidays too, because it usually meant that she got two Easters. The Greek Orthodox Church celebrates its Easter usually one week after the Catholic Easter. And Greek Easter at her uncle and aunt's house was always one of the best days. I am grateful for them providing that and for being able to experience such a strong family bond. Even a few years after their son Christos died, they still celebrate Easter with family and friends.

Father's Day. Just one year prior, Zoi had created one of the most precious gifts I've ever received from her — a handmade Father's Day card. In it, she goes into intricate details about "What is a father?" to her. This card is filled with love, respect, enlightenment, music, understanding, clarity, and appreciation of our relationship as father and daughter. And even though this was a hand-written, hand-drawn card, Zoi often drew other pictures and gave them to me as gifts too. This holiday affected me the most as I was reminded that Zoi and I are always connected. Every time I read that card, I know how special Zoi really is.

I approached celebrating Memorial Day, the 4th of July and Labor Day more as long weekends this first year. For some, these holidays may be just as tough because your loved one is not around. I'm not discounting them at all. Everyone's journey is different.

We were approaching Zoi's birthday in October. I knew it was going to be a real challenge for all of the family and her friends. Like the other holidays we navigated in these first months, again I felt compelled to create new memories for this particularly very difficult day. Ahead of the date, Maria and I coordinated going to Salem with Christos to go visit Arminda. When I got to Maria's house that morning, Maria was outside. I got out of my car, we walked toward each other, and we embraced and cried. It was hard for all of us. When we arrived at Arminda's apartment, I got a text from Arminda's cousin saying we should join her and her uncle and aunt's family over at the local marina. They were out on their boat for the day and had come in and docked for a couple of hours. It was a really beautiful day. There were a few clouds in the sky and it was warm out. On the boat, it was nice just being connected to everyone. About an hour in, a single storm cloud came in over the bay. In a flash, a downpour erupted right over the boat. Maria and I were outside just standing in the rain. We didn't care. A few minutes passed and off in the distance, the most beautiful rainbow appeared. It was amazing because it appeared from that single rain cloud. There were no other clouds around. Maria, Arminda and I began to cry. To me, it was Zoi saying "Hi" to us on her birthday.

The hardest holidays to navigate besides birthdays and anniversaries are Thanksgiving and Christmas. The previous Thanksgiving had been at my house with both girls and my parents. That was the last time my mom and dad saw Zoi before she died. For this first Thanksgiving after, Arminda and I went to visit Scott and his family at his sister Cory's house in Arkansas. We flew to Hobbs, New Mexico, where Scott lived, and then drove to Little Rock, Arkansas the next day. It was an amazing 13-hour drive through Texas and into Arkansas. We spent the next few days doing nothing but reconnecting and, honestly, being lazy. The day of Thanksgiving was good up until we were about to sit down and eat. At that point, both Arminda and I lost it. We just cried because we missed Zoi so much on that day. These 'firsts' are so tough.

Christmas came up quickly too. I had been putting off even decorating. In my mind, I was questioning why I even needed to. Finally, the weekend before Christmas, it hit me that I needed to do something. Zoi would have wanted that to be the case. I got a surge of energy and I went upstairs and grabbed the four-foot fake tree I had used the previous eight Christmases, along with boxes of decorations. When I opened the boxes, I started to cry immediately. Inside, it was like looking into a time capsule. I had forgotten about all of the handmade decorations that the girls had made over the years. I was filled with mixed emotions as I set up a very limited Christmas.

As the one-year anniversary of Zoi's death approached, I didn't want it go by without any acknowledgement. It had been hard for all of the family and her friends that past year. I wanted to keep it simple. That morning, I went up to see Arminda. Later, I invited some of Zoi's friends over for pizza and soda and we just sat and talked about Zoi. It really felt like she was there with us in many ways, yet it was also hard to fathom that she was no longer with us physically. In all, we came together and the energy in the room was beautiful.

For anyone who has lost a spouse, your wedding anniversary will be a tough day to navigate. Remember the good times that you had and what you loved to do together, and go and do something like that again on that day, for you! Because it will honor your spouse. I know it will be hard and the tendency is to not do anything, but there will be some joy found in the day. At the very least you will not have let your grief get the better of you.

MAPS:

Mindful — This was all brand new and I have to give myself a break to "breathe" through each day, especially the holidays and anniversaries.

Approach — We will get through these holidays and anniversaries. Zoi would want us to keep going and be happy. And if it was me that had died, I would want Zoi to be happy as well.

Predict — I see each holiday and anniversary as an opportunity to create a new memory.

Suck — These days are going to be difficult, but we will all get through them.

18

How are others doing?

Zoi had been hospitalized on a couple of occasions when she was working through the rough spots. Though she hated every minute of being in a hospital, she would make the best of it by making new friends really fast. When I would go and visit her, she would always introduce me as "Dad" and her friends would always say "Hi Zoi's dad!" It was one of the sweetest things that Zoi did. It gave me comfort to know there were others around her, including the counselors, who cared. And Zoi always surrounded herself with people that loved deeply. After Zoi's death, it became natural for me to reach out to Zoi's friends and check in on them. Some of them still said "Hi Zoi's dad!" when they greeted me.

I didn't know of Harry personally when Zoi was in the hospital. I would visit Zoi most nights, even if it was for just a short period of time. And after Zoi died, I don't remember hearing from Harry, but his mom would reach out. As time passed, I got to know Harry better, along with another of Zoi's friends, Danielle (Danni). Since Zoi was such a connector and an immediate friend to so many, she loved it when other kids connected with her too. Zoi had a very deep and irreverent sense of humor, and she used this often as a way to connect with her friends who were having a hard time.

A few months after Zoi died, both Danni and Harry reached out on Facebook. They wanted to see how I was doing, and it was just as important to me to see how they were doing. We made plans to meet up to visit Zoi's resting place. Both Danni and Harry came with their moms. We had lunch first and it gave Danni and Harry time to catch up. I talked a bit with their moms and then we headed over to the cemetery. It was an awesome and sunny early summer day.

Harry then asked if he could play his ukulele for Zoi. I honestly hadn't heard a ukulele since Zoi's death. And he played "Home" by Edward Sharpe and the Magnetic Zeroes for her. I lost it. It was the song that Zoi used to play for Harry when they were in the hospital when he was having a hard time. It was so beautiful and Harry did such a great job. Then he played a song that he had written for Zoi, aptly called "Zoi's Song." In it, Harry recounts his experience with Zoi while they were in the unit and lets her know that she did so much for him. He just recalls all around the awesomeness of Zoi, and how she touched his world in so many ways.

Afterward, eyes puffy from crying, I asked the two of them to really understand how important it was for them to be "here" now. I told them that they mattered so very much and that they aren't done yet. There is a purpose for being here. "I can talk to you, now, and say these things to you," and I pointed down to the ground and said, "I can't talk to her anymore. I say this with love. Don't give up on you. You are destined for great things and this is only a temporary situation you are in now." After we shared some more tears, we also shared some pics and hugs, and left.

I connected with Zoi's other friends too, and would try to check in with them weekly, sometimes more than once a week. A lot of them didn't know what to make of this situation. They would say that my strength was their source of strength to get through this — knowing that if I could keep going, so could they. I would tell them that they too were my strength. "We are in this together and we will all get through this together." I felt that, collectively, they all reminded me of Zoi, each one possessing some trait that Zoi used to express and that I love about her. That is not to say that if one of her friends didn't have something that reminded me of Zoi that I wouldn't check in on them too, but rather that each one of these kids has a power within.

MAPS:

Mindful — Friends and family are trying to navigate the loss of Zoi.

Approach — We are all in this together and we will get through it together.

Predict — The heartache will eventually be replaced with heart song as they remember more of the good times than the bad times.

Suck — It's so hard that she's not here, but she would want us to truly live and be happy.

19

What is my purpose now?

hat the hell? I said this out loud as I stood in the doorway of Zoi's bedroom one morning a few months after she died. I was irate! I had woken up about an hour earlier, had my breakfast, let the dog out, and was getting ready for work. I stopped in her doorway just to look in, and it ALL hit me at one time — holy crap, she wasn't here anymore! Holy crap, she's not coming back! Holy crap, how can I ever disturb her bedroom? What am I going to do with all of her things?!

WHAT THE HELL, ZOI?! I broke down crying and a flood of other questions came rolling in all at once. I collected myself after about 15 minutes and made my way out the door to work for the day.

I didn't want to brush off what had happened earlier, so after work I sat outside on my deck and started to write down some notes:

Without glossing over the biggest question of them all, the reason "why" someone died — we may never know fully why — I instead began to consider that if we focus on healing ourselves and then helping others, life takes on a new meaning for us. When we do that, the "why" of our loved one's death shifts to a more important question: Why am I here? Differently asked, what is my greater purpose, and do I have one? Hell yes, you do! So, great, how do I find that in the fog of this loss?

Two years and eight months after Zoi died, I attended a leadership event in Tampa, Florida led by former Green Beret, (Ret.) Lieutenant Col. Scott Mann. While this leadership event focused on teaching us how to bridge the gaps in a society where trust has eroded, and how to connect with others deeply and authentically, most of us took to the specific lesson of finding our greater purpose, or "tracks" as Scott calls it.

One of Scott's greater purposes (tracks) is to help warriors find their voice and tell their story in transition from military service to civilian service, to defeat violent extremists, and to teach 'rooftop leadership' to civilians. You may be asking, what are these tracks that I keep mentioning? The tracks you leave are your *legacy*. It's the impact and imprint you make in this world now and long after you have left.

Scott shared with us that back in 2007, his father Rex had stage IV non-Hodgkin's lymphoma. Scott was having a very difficult time seeing his father in such a deteriorated state, especially when it looked like Rex wasn't going to survive. Scott told his father that he wasn't ready for him to die yet. Rex said, "I've left my tracks, son." Fortunately, Rex did survive his treatment. He told me of his tracks in a one-on-one conversation we had recently. "One of my tracks is to restore the American chestnut tree." In his mid 70s, Rex is still traveling around the country speaking and teaching on the importance of preserving this great American icon. And you know what, he's building a movement to make this happen. His tracks will serve long after he dies. The same goes for the tracks you and I leave; they will always serve, now and well after we die. After Rex was invited to the White House by former President George W. Bush, and spoke to the President about the American chestnut tree, one was planted on the White House property. Rex works to teach others this concept as well.

At the Tampa event, we wrote our tracks as if a loved one were holding our hand as we take our last breath. And then 15 years later, our loved one is sitting with a friend and that friend asks about us. We write our tracks by asking, what would we want our loved ones to say about us to others? What legacy do you want to leave?

I'll share a few of the answers I wrote down at this event:

1. He did so much for others in healing.
2. He helped many people to overcome loss.
3. He was a light and hope for people through the fog of loss.
4. He recognized the capacity in all of us to heal.

From that exercise, I was able to derive my true purpose:

- To help people overcome loss and see the beauty in life again.
- To build resilience leaders.
- To help people navigate struggle, surpass survival mode, and live!

You never know who you'll reach with your tracks and purpose. It's always something that is much bigger than we are. As Rex would say, "Just a small thing that you do for another person, that you may not think that much of, can mean the world to that person — it could change a life!" What tracks do you want to leave? In section III of this book, we'll work on establishing your tracks and how this will help you find your greater purpose, too.

MAPS:

Mindful — I want to find my greater purpose.

Approach — Finding my purpose will be a challenge, but the alternative of not pursuing my purpose is not living into my birthright.

Predict — I step into a new greater purpose to serve others — to pick up Zoi's torch.

Suck — Making an impact with my purpose is not going to be easy. Leadership is clunky.

20

What's next in my life?

For quite a while after Zoi died, and as I was navigating this new "normal," I wondered what was next in my life. Grieving is a vortex, and you rarely feel grounded or centered. So expecting to know what was next in life right away was putting undue pressure on me. For some, their next chapter is revealed relatively quickly and for others, like me, it may take some time. I didn't put a timeline on figuring it out.

Eventually, I figured I would dive back into my health and fitness coaching business. It was something that I had been doing before Zoi died and I had loved it. I also started to pay more attention to my personal development training, and then I discovered that helping others really hit home.

This personal development training lead me to some really great new friends and mentors whom I'm grateful for in so many ways. It's helped to strengthen the bonds of my family and other friends and it's showed me that above all, life goes on.

MAPS:

Mindful — It will take some getting used to being in this new "normal."

Approach — I don't necessarily have to have my next thing or my life figured out right away. I had to grieve first.

Predict — A focus on others first, and then my next chapter will manifest itself.

Suck — I am impatient, but it will take time.

21

How am I ever going to move on from this?

When we are grieving, there is a natural tendency to want to turn the clock back — to go back. But instead of focusing on what we can't change, we can take the temperature of where we are today and then where we want to be. But how do we move on while still honoring the person who died? It begins with forgiveness and making peace.

I worked in Boston for four years. I would take the commuter rail from Norwood to Boston each day for work. I had only been working in Boston for about three months when Zoi died and it took me some time to get back into the swing of things, as you can imagine. About one year later I found myself stuck and unable to move on.

When the train returned me to Norwood each night, I would get in to my car and drive the two miles home. However, at about mile one I would start crying and would ask Zoi for forgiveness. This ritual continued for many weeks until one day I got off the train, got into my car and the second the door closed, I broke down. Great! Now I had two miles to cry. By the time I reached mile one I was sobbing and having a difficult time seeing where I was going. The windows were fogged up, the radio was off and I just wanted to get home. The traffic was unbelievably heavy that day too.

I started to ask Zoi for forgiveness, actually beg her for it. "I'm so sorry, pumpkins. I should have been stronger for you. I'm so so sorry, child. Please forgive me." And as if she was sitting in the seat next to me in the car, I thought about her saying to me, "I'm OK dad, jeez. Stop it!" In that moment, the tears turned to laughter, because I knew I had been stuck and this was not serving me or anyone around me in the way of healing. Plus, it was a dope slap from Zoi for me to chill out!

Later, at home, I sat down and was trying to recall the clarity of Zoi's voice and what I had heard. I needed to make peace with what was. The longer that I held onto that pattern of sobbing and begging for forgiveness, the harder it would be to move forward. So the next day, I did something different for the two-mile trip home from the train station: I put on the radio station that she used to listen to and jammed out to songs by Nirvana, Foo Fighters and the Red Hot Chili Peppers. In traffic, with the windows rolled down, I sang along. It felt so different to approach this drive home from a new perspective. It showed me that until I made peace with Zoi's loss, forgave myself and forgave her,

I was going to be stuck.

MAPS:

Mindful — Although I was stuck and blaming myself, I knew I didn't want to stay here for long.

Approach — This was difficult, but finding a way through was the only way to go.

Predict — I envisioned a time and place when this wouldn't hurt so much.

Suck — Blaming myself was not serving me or anyone I knew in the way of healing. I had to make peace with Zoi's death.

22

How am I going to get back to my work?

When Zoi died, I was (and will be always) grateful that I had the support of my boss Jason and the company to take as much time as I needed to sort through it. I had been working at the company for only a few months when Zoi died, and yet they gave me the runway I needed to grieve. They never pressured me to come back sooner than when I was ready to. I know not everyone has that space available to them. Whether you work for a company as an employee or you own your own company, either way, getting support in your leave from the office is essential to your healing process.

So how do you deal with getting back to work after the death of a loved one? Some people find solace in their work and return right away. For them, the busier they are, it works for them. Others dread the thought of returning to work and can't, for many months. And sometimes, people quit altogether to focus on themselves and their family. I'm not suggesting that any of these three are the right choice for you; instead I encourage you to find the right path for your situation. If you are grieving a loss and you feel that you're OK to return to work, that's OK too. Feeling OK to carry on does not mean that you don't care about your family or the loved one that you lost. It means that you, and only you, are the one at the helm of your life. Go with it! It's OK! There may be times when it ebbs and flows, but it's all about taking the temperature and doing what works for you. There is no timeline for grief, and being pressured to go back into a work situation can slow down or even stop your grieving process. If you are struggling with this, speaking with a mental health professional and coming up with a plan for your return to work is essential. He or she can help assess your level of readiness for this transition.

In a Forbes.com article titled "Returning to Work After the Devastating Loss of a Loved One," writer David K. Williams writes about the loss of David Goldberg, husband of Facebook COO Sheryl Sandberg, and how this death tugged at his heart after losing his own 25-year-old son, Cameron, to stomach cancer. David talks about regaining his "work rhythm" after his son died. "Returning to work after the death of a loved one is difficult, and it's a challenge that's renewed year after year." David also spoke with Jason Garner, the former CEO of Global Music at Live Nation. Garner also experienced the loss of his mother, to stomach cancer. But Garner's loss gave him a "new lens" with which to see the world through. Garner goes on to describe how this new lens let him find and make peace with losing his mother. "Death is such an intimate experience…it's especially personal because it invites us — forces us — to look in the mirror, to examine our crowded lives, and to question the meaning of it all," said Garner.

I couldn't agree more! Not only do we need the time to heal, but we are creatures who seek meaning, and when something as intimate and personal as the death of a loved one hits us, we all have the ability to reflect on what this means to us, and to find our own pathway and tools for our journey back to better days. Sometimes, though, we struggle and we stay stuck. Later in this section I'll talk about being stuck and its effects on us.

Garner goes on to share that "Death really is an invitation to open our hearts, to experience the feelings of pain and grief, and then to honor our loved ones by going back into the world with an open heart to do our work with an increased awareness and compassion for our needs and the needs of others."

When the time was right for me to return to the office, I was ready, and it was a healthy distraction. Staying inside at home was difficult, but I could only handle about three days in the office per week for the first couple of months. Given that this is a difficult process for anyone who has experienced loss, where work is coming back into focus, there are three things that I believe can help you in this transitional time.

The first is to feel the emotions of the loss. Pushing them down only to stay strong for others is like trying to put a piece of gum in the crack of a dam — you will burst too. So instead, give yourself permission to feel, to cry, whatever it is that you need to emote. The key is to give yourself permission to feel.

For example, I found that giving myself the permission to mourn helped tremendously. I gave myself a one- to two-hour "ritual" in the morning to feel the pain to help me get it out. Eventually, I didn't cry every morning, even though I had given myself permission to do so. Everyone will approach this differently. Set a timeframe and give yourself permission to do this. Maybe you say to yourself, "I will cry when I feel like I need to and for as long as I need to, for one week straight — no restrictions. But at the end of that week, I now must focus on something else." It's really important to honor the timeframe you set; you will find that releasing that energy literally is like making the waters (the emotions) behind the "dam" subside.

The second thing to help you transition back to work is to know that it is OK to smile again, and at any time during your grieving. I remember the first belly laugh that I had, and it was only days after Zoi died. Immediately afterward I thought it was strange that I laughed like that when I had been crying my eyes out just a few hours earlier. I felt guilty too, but I resolved that it was something that was funny and it was OK to laugh. Hell, it broke the tension! There are other emotions that come flooding in, and it's OK to feel those too. You are not dishonoring someone by smiling and laughing and having moments of being "OK." It's being human. Laughter may also be a great coping mechanism.

Lastly, the best way to transition is to heal at your own pace. One question I hear all the time is "Why am I not healing fast enough?" Comparing your grieving process to anyone else's is counterproductive to your own healing. I recently read about a woman who lost her son to a car accident. Thirty days later she was upset that she didn't feel better. It is in these times when we must give ourselves a break and realize that this is a process that has no timeline. When the time is right, we can make peace with our loss. When the time is right, we will begin to feel better. And when the time is right, you will be OK. At the time of the writing of this book, it's been three and a half years since Zoi's death, and I love her as much now as I did the day she was born. Love never dies. If you find that that you're not sure about your grieving process, or do not feel like you're able to ever heal, please seek connections with friends, family, support groups, therapists — anyone who can be that sounding board for you and help you find your own peace of mind.

MAPS:

Mindful — Returning to work was going to be a challenge.

Approach — I needed space to grieve, and was going to take care of myself during this process. If I didn't, I couldn't focus on others.

Predict — When I am ready to return to work, I'll be able to give my all again in my career role.

Suck — Going back to work full time will be difficult, but it supports my family, it keeps a roof over my head and food on the table.

23

Are they OK?

I pondered whether Zoi was "OK" for months after she died. I was increasingly frustrated, sad and I wanted answers. None came. I would constantly ask "Zoi, are you OK?" That silence just sucks. My therapist had given me a book called *Proof of Heaven* by Dr. Eben Alexander. In it, Dr. Alexander goes into intricate detail about his near-death experience and how even in a coma, he had the experience of what he calls "heaven." He attempts to provide us with as much story, knowledge and understanding of what he experienced as he can. When I say he attempts this, it's because he admits several times in the book that his words cannot fully express what he experienced in this place of pure love.

Dr. Alexander's second book, *The Map of Heaven*, is a deeper dive into why our loved ones are not truly gone, but rather have taken a different form of energy and exist on a different plane that we cannot comprehend as conscious, living beings. This book was also very helpful and I finished it in early May 2015, right before I had to go to Los Angeles for a work trade show.

The trip would be my very first time in L.A. I was excited to go to California as I had dreamed about it for many years. How cool would it be to see the Hollywood sign, or visit Venice Beach and Santa Monica…maybe even Malibu? When we arrived, the first impression of L.A. was that I could get very used to the 75 degrees and sun every day.

Fantasizing aside, reality steps in and you realize that you are there for work purposes. The 14-hour days prepping for the trade show don't leave you much time to get out and sightsee. After one of the nights of setting up, my coworkers and I did get down to Hermosa Beach, just south of L.A. to visit a couple of mutual friends. Taking in a true Pacific sunset was epic. When they say that the sun seems to hang in the sky, they aren't lying. I was feeling what California was all about. It was beautiful.

The trade show was a success and a few days later we packed up in a fraction of the time it took us to set up. I had offered to stay in L.A. one additional day to confirm that everything had shipped back to Boston. I woke up the next morning with a text from our event leader to tell me that it was going to be my responsibility to get the rental car back to LAX because he didn't have time to do so on his way out. At first I was pissed. Why leave me with this responsibility? But then I realized that I had a fully paid-for, gassed-up rental that I could use for a day in L.A. and had no timeline for that day once I confirmed the boxes and crates had left for Boston. I hadn't been able to check out L.A. or put my feet in the Pacific Ocean on this trip, so this was a great opportunity to do so. I drove to the coast and I pulled into the parking lot of Santa Monica Beach right off the Pacific Coast Highway. Given that this was early May, I had been told that there is a term for a specific weather pattern called "May gray / June gloom": it's overcast for most of the day along the coast and sometimes, it burns off and you get the California sun. This was one of those days. It was warm (about 70 degrees) but very overcast. My goal though, was to get a rock for Zoi's room.

When Zoi and Arminda were little, we used to go to Duxbury Beach in Massachusetts. It was the same place that I took Zoi in 2012 to clear her head. When the girls were little, we went year-round. In the summers, they played for the entire day. In the winter, we would just love how quiet the beach was except for the sounds of waves crashing on the shore. No matter the time of year though, we would always bring home some rocks from Duxbury. Colored rocks, opaque white rocks, certain shaped rocks — anything that struck us, we grabbed. Now whenever I travel, I make it a point to pick up a rock from that destination, bring it back and put it up in Zoi's room. Santa Monica Beach was the ideal place for me to find the rock from this L.A. trip.

If you've ever been to the Santa Monica beach, you know that it is huge! Not just in length, but also in depth. In one direction, you see the Malibu mountains hugging the coast and in the other direction, you see the Santa Monica Pier. The cool thing was on this day, I had the entire beach to myself.

I started to walk toward the water and look for rocks. The problem was, there are very few if any rocks on that beach to begin with. Every couple hundred feet I would look up and just take in what my eyes were seeing. I felt very peaceful there and I kept saying to Zoi, "I wish you were here, pumpkins. I know you would love it." I walked for about five minutes and finally found a rock. I picked it up and put it in my pocket. I changed direction and walked for another few minutes before I found another rock and also put it in my pocket. I did this for a little while longer before I found a couple more rocks and a handful of tiny clamshells. All of them went in my pocket. I made my way down by the water. Waves crashing in front of me, I put my hands and feet in the surf that washed up, and just took it all in. It was emotional just being there. It was surreal that this was on the complete opposite coast from where I used to bring the girls. The wind was blowing and it was warm. It was hard to believe that I was experiencing this and Zoi wasn't able to. I took a few more pics and headed back to the car to head back to the hotel.

When I got into my room I took the rocks and shells out of my pocket and placed them on the desk, and something struck me. They seemed to form a shape. I took two of the rocks and adjusted them, and I sat down in disbelief. The rocks spelled the name "Zoi." I broke down crying. I wasn't crying because Zoi wasn't with me that day. I cried because she *was* there with me, connecting and communicating as only she could. You can see the picture that I took in the hotel room that morning in the back of this book.

In that moment, I recalled the chapter "Gifts" from *The Map of Heaven*, where Dr. Alexander tells us that our loved ones do leave us gifts, and we have the ability to see these if we want to, and are open to it. This was a tremendous gift from Zoi and it showed me that she is ever connected to everything on this earth. Like you and I know where everything is in our homes, how it is furnished, locations of every appliance, every picture and trinket, so too does Zoi know about every blade of grass, every tree, every grain of sand and every rock that is on this planet. I believe that Zoi led me to those rocks on the beach. And it ratified my belief that Zoi *is* OK, and that she does exist on another plane. This belief may not be shared by everyone who reads this book, but I'm sharing my experiences with you and what I believe my connection to Zoi still is.

MAPS:

Mindful — I wanted to believe Zoi was OK.

Approach — I had expected that Zoi and I would be communicating openly. I had to be open to other forms of communication.

Predict — Eventually I would open my eyes to the signs.

Suck — The silence sucks, and you will never hear your loved one's voice again. It doesn't mean you can't connect in other ways.

24

Did I do enough? What could I have done more of?

One summer day in 2016 I was traveling up to Maine with my dog Bean to visit my mom and dad for a long weekend. I flipped on the 'Alternative' music radio station that Zoi used to listen to, and a song that she used to sing along to came on. Instantly I was taken back to when the song came out in the early '90s and what life was like back then. I imagined hearing Zoi's voice singing again. It was a warm feeling of love and pride. Always is, even to this day.

Then other thoughts came in — what about the time I missed an opportunity to handle a situation with Zoi better? Or, what if I had approached reprimanding her differently? What if I had gone and visited her one more time in the hospital? What if? What if? Ugh! My thoughts shifted once more to "Oh my God, did I do enough for her? What if I didn't? What if I had done more when she was here? Maybe she would still be here or things would be different."

Because of our loss, we could feel that we should have done more. A new mother asks if she did enough when her baby dies at 30 days old without any warning. A military commander asks this when they send their men and women into conflict and some don't come back alive. A mom asks this when her son dies in a car accident. A wife asks this if her husband dies of cancer at home with hospice care. Death is a part of life. It doesn't take our loved ones out of spite or to hurt us, it is simply its nature. But I believe that to answer that question "Did I do enough? What could I have done more of?" there are three things that can help you gain clarity and confidence that you *did* do enough.

The first thing is that we must find a way to not only forgive our loved ones for dying, but also forgive ourselves for what we perceive we "didn't do" for them. When I was going through this process, every injury or sickness that Zoi ever had felt like it was AMPLIFIED and it tugged at my heart, with sadness and with so much pressure. When I forgave myself that I had done the best that I could do at that time, which is all any of us can do, then the pressure subsided considerably. This is one of the best gifts we can give ourselves in our grief.

Secondly, we must make peace with the loss of our loved one. When I made peace with Zoi's death, and also with "what was," I began to open up to gratitude for "what is" in my life — like Zoi's sister Arminda, and her brother Christos. I had gratitude that Zoi's mom brought her into this world. Most importantly, I had gratitude that Zoi was here for the 15 years that I got to be, and still am, her dad. I was grateful for my dog Bean, the roof over my head, food on my table, my family and friends, all of it! My heart is warming up just writing this out. I invite you to actively write down just three things daily that you are grateful for too. It can be anything – the universe, your home, your family, your pets, taco Tuesday. Who cares, right? It's for *you* and no one else can tell you what to be grateful for. Nothing can ever replace your loved one, but gratitude opens your heart to what is good in your life today. It's very powerful.

Lastly, accepting that we *did* do as much as we could for our loved one, as hard as it may be, is liberating. This ties into forgiving ourselves and making peace with the loss. Acceptance is giving ourselves permission to be OK. The Buddha said, "Everything that has a beginning, has an ending. Make your peace with that and all will be well."

MAPS:

Mindful — I was feeling I didn't do enough for Zoi while she was here.

Approach — If I had died and Zoi was asking me the same question, "Did I do enough?", I would definitely say yes.

Predict — Accepting that I did do enough will be liberating.

Suck — We can't turn back the clock to fix anything, but we did do enough.

25

Will I ever feel better?

"Eric, I don't know if I'll ever feel better." This is what a friend texted me a few weeks ago after the loss of her father. She had been taking care of him and although it was exhausting for her, all of it stopped suddenly when he died of complications. One minute she's running errands trying to make sure he's got all of his medications, that the nurses are scheduled to come to their house for treatment, and that his food is prepared properly. The next minute, he's gone. They had a good relationship and she missed him terribly. She often sought his counsel on difficult life issues and despite being sick, his mind remained sharp. "You will feel better, but it takes work. I'm not talking about labor intensive, I'm talking about internal work that's approached with love and care of your self." This was my response to her.

Inside the fog of grief, it's hard to comprehend how we will ever feel better. Sometimes, it's all consuming, but there is a way through. Here are some indicators of when you will be feeling better. They are not in order:

- When you start to answer *your* questions authentically.
- When you forgive and make peace with the person you lost.
- When you are grateful for what is in your life.
- When survival is recognized as a milestone, not a destination.
- When you frame your mindset that this is happening for you, not to you.
- When you function and live with intention, and take care of yourself.
- When you form core values and beliefs that drive the direction of your life.
- When you never give up.
- When you keep going.

"If you're going through hell, keep going." —Winston Churchill.

26

How can I help a friend or family member who is struggling?

Truly listening to others is hard. I work on that daily and probably will for the rest of my life. I still make mistakes with this. I constantly ask myself, "When was the last time that we actively listened to what someone was sharing with us without interruption?" If you think about how most of us listen, usually we are waiting for the other person to finish their sentence so that we can quickly speak our mind. That can create distrust and/or a lack of empathy. When we actively listen to others, especially those who are grieving, we build trust and empathy between us and the other person. You are then more valued for having truly listened to what they had to say.

When we are grieving or know someone who is grieving, the subject of a loss may come up in conversation. For some, it may be very difficult to talk about it, and there is no obligation to do so. In any conversation, we may hear or say, "I can't even imagine." The intent of that statement is to ease pain, but the person saying it is putting him- or herself into a mental scenario of that same pain. Our brains cannot differentiate between real or imagined trauma. Meaning, even if we just learn of a personal trauma, whether ours or someone else's, our brains are wired to imagine we too are experiencing the same trauma. It's a protection mechanism that stems from the "fight or flight" limbic system in our brain.

Death is a difficult life experience. It is an element of the human condition and at some point in our lives all of us are going to experience the loss of a loved one. Supporting someone who is grieving by listening, connecting and being empathetic is possible without it being draining to you or feeling like you have to take on their pain. So how do we help? What do we say?

First, a reflection of feeling goes a long way. For example, after learning of Zoi's death one of my mentors said to me, "I'm so sorry for your loss. I'm sure this is difficult for you and it sucks." By reflecting my feelings back to me, it made me feel like he truly cared about me and my family, because yeah, it did suck! It also allowed me to share more deeply with him because I trusted him further. He then followed up with a stronger statement of support. "I may not be able to fully understand how hard this is for you, and nothing can take away this pain, but I'm proud of how you are dealing with this. I'm not sure I could do it."

Second, our presence and availability for the person or family in grief is so very helpful. Simply saying "If you need anything, let me know" is a nice gesture, but when people are grieving they need to know that true family and friends will be with them and in whatever capacity that is possible. When we ask the person who is grieving what they need for support, it can be difficult for them to articulate. Yes, we do have our lives to live as well and timing can be challenging, but in the fog of loss, the griever's thoughts can be blurred by the stress. Taking the temperature of the situation and also speaking with other family members and friends to coordinate your presence can make a huge difference.

Lastly, offering resources that helped you in your time of need or when you were grieving is very helpful. When my therapist gave me the book Proof of Heaven, she thought it would help me. And it did. The timing of receiving that resource was perfect. Have you been a member of any support groups, or do you know any that provide value? Are there websites that helped you? Are there books or movies that helped you? Note: Please take into consideration when sharing these resources that the person who is grieving may not be ready to take in this information just yet. Ask questions and converse, and if they are searching for resources, this would be a good time to offer yours.

27

What is the timeline for healing?

"…It feels like if I'm resilient, I'm not grieving enough. It's as if I must not have loved [my husband] enough because I'm not more of a mess. And that hurts. It makes me feel guilty. A therapist just told me that being resilient doesn't mean I'm not in pain, and I'm not grieving. But she didn't tell me HOW to go about correcting this!" This is what Mary T. posted in an online forum recently.

Everyone processes grief differently. When we own our grieving process, no one can tell us how to feel or when it's time to stop grieving. Being resilient is good. You don't owe any explanations of how you feel. Letting others question how much you loved someone is not conducive to healing either. I don't know what Mary's situation was at home. However, yes, she is grieving her own way and yes, it's

OK for her to feel what she feels WHEN she feels it. I replied to Mary's post with words of encouragement to focus on her healing, as that was most important. Also, that grieving takes many forms and there is no one single way to get through the storm. Nor is there a timeline. You may feel guilty and may be embarrassed for feeling OK some of the time. You may feel better sooner rather than later, too. Frankly, it's no one else's business. As Eleanor Roosevelt said, "No one can make you feel inferior without your consent."

28

Why am I here and they are not? I feel stuck.

Coming out of the fog of a loss is, well, just weird. Nothing makes sense about what happened and yet, you are functioning. The previous questions are just some of the ones that I know of and I know there are many more out there to be answered by each of us. We have to make peace with *what was*, so that we can become grateful for *what is*. Then our world begins to open up, and our blockages start to shift into beams of light — of hope for us and our future. Making peace with the loss is OK. Feeling better, smiling again, forgiving yourself, are *all* OK. It can feel weird to feel OK. We all process grief differently, so there is no right way or wrong way. It's your way.

It was months before I felt somewhat normal. I wasn't eating well and I wasn't exercising at all. I just wasn't myself. It was the grief that was gripping me. Do you ever have those dreams where you want to run, but no matter how much you try, you're almost just running in place? When I had those dreams, I realized that I was literally (and metaphorically) stuck. And it took a long time for me to accept it and let it really sink in that Zoi would not like it if she knew I was letting all of those good memories from her life stop me from living mine. Being stuck was keeping me from healing further. Some people remain "stuck" after any loss in life. And by stuck, I'm not talking about never finding another relationship or another job. I'm talking about carrying the load on their shoulders that they will never feel better or truly make peace with what was. And that gravity carries heavily into their future. It weighs them down to the point where they can't walk on any pathway back to better days. Some contend with this for months, if not years. Some even for the rest of their lives.

And look, I get it. I've been there. When I got divorced, I was stuck for a very long time. It kept me from living in the present moment, and I lost precious time with Zoi and Arminda because my energy was going elsewhere. I know the challenges that exist with loss and being stuck. It denies us access to our greater purpose. It denies us happiness. And most of all it denies us thriving in life.

When you take your last breath, do you want that to be a short breath of regret, or a very deep breath that you did everything possible and fought for your life despite the losses? That you fought to thrive in resilience? The direction we go in life should not be dictated by what sets us back, but rather by what pushes us forward. To get unstuck, we have to replace the regrets and sad memories and move toward a place of healing. In other words, we have to work on removing these blockages from our lives so that we too can thrive. Knowing the challenge that exists with removing these blockages, we tend to want a quick fix and get frustrated when that doesn't work. Thus, we feel like nothing is going to change! We have to move through our struggles to heal.

Death does not offer us the ability to find the reasons "why" our loved one died. Nor does it offer any type of recovery from the loss. That's not death's job. Its job, its energy, is to transition the living to the afterworld (or wherever you may believe the energy goes). Death does not have to provide you with any reasons or tell you ahead of time. It just has to do its job. But what death also doesn't tell you is that it has to leave something behind as part of the deal for taking your loved one. These things left behind, I affectionately call gifts or tools of resilience. So how does someone find these gifts or tools, especially when it seems like it won't be helpful? The good news is, these tools will always have a place to be helpful, at the right time.

Throughout all of the stages of grief — sadness, anger, frustration, confusion, pain, guilt, etc. — the only way that you can find the gifts left to you by death is to know that they exist, to know that you have the ability to look for, find and take in these gifts. Also, to know that any and all of the good qualities and strengths you may have are gifts you possess *right now* to help you along your journey.

Rex Mann laments that he taught his sons, "You're not allowed to quit. If it's something worth pursuing, you will get knocked on your ass. You'll grieve, and you may feel sorry for yourself — go sit on a stump and think about it before getting up and moving on." Feeling self-pity and guilt denies us access to our greater purpose. It denies us happiness. And most of all, it doesn't honor the person we've lost. So, if you're stuck and you're asking yourself "Now what?", take the time to grieve (sitting on a stump) that you need to take, but also work to find the light and hope in your life (getting up and moving on). Doing this has changed my life and I know it can change yours too! Life has always gone on. We've created an artificial concept of death — that it's devastating. Death is a natural part of life; it just sometimes happens out of the order we expect it to. That's not to suggest that we walk around afraid of death and/or wait for it to come knocking on our door. No, we must LIVE life to the fullest starting today, without wasting a single breath, and now to *find* the gifts that death left behind.

29

What if I don't want to be in grief? And why exploring these questions helps you along your journey.

hen I set out to write this book about the journey and needing guidance along the way, the vision I kept seeing in my head was that

W of me hiking along a long dirt road or path. In this vision, it's dusk, around the time when the sun throws its most beautiful colors against the backdrop of trees, mountains and the clouds above. I'm walking, but I've also got this sense that I'm being guided. As I proceed on the journey I find myself on a long open straight section of the path. I stop for a quick breather. And I look back just long enough to see where I've been thus far, not only on this new journey, but also my life overall.

Have you ever been hiking on a long trail or mountain and you stop and try to see down through the trees from where you started? It's hard to see that origin point above the tree line. And you might even say to yourself, "Damn, I've come a long way… more than I thought I had." How much different does the world look from that vantage point? There is a sense of accomplishment for that part of the journey — our current journey through grief. It's the combination of the miles you've walked already and the questions you've asked and worked to answer. "Is the clarity of my questions keeping me aligned with my journey, and what tracks am I leaving for others to learn from and follow? How can I move forward on this journey, have I done enough? Are they OK, and what are others thinking of me as I take this journey?" All of this matters.

As I stand there and catch my breath, I recall all of the previous times I had to stop along the journey to catch my breath or pitch camp — sometimes due to injury (mental and physical), and other times due to my own reasons for stopping, including asking the above questions. These camping stops allow me to collect myself and reflect on not only where I've been, but also on where I'm going from there. It becomes clear that each time I stopped, another tool appeared in my backpack (another question answered) because it formed out of the self-reflection, hard work and miles I've walked.

Answering these questions is the beginning stage of this journey back to better days. The tools in our backpack for the journey moving forward. However, as we continue to navigate this path, we need something more to help us, right? We need the essential building blocks of resilience in order to thrive again. We are meaning-seeking creatures and it's in our nature to truly live. Let's explore what it takes to move out of survival mode and live with intention.

PART III

Coming Out of the Fog

"If you love life, don't waste time, for time is what life is made up of."
— Bruce Lee

30

Zoi's tracks

"Eric. I am so very sorry for your loss. I want you to know that Zoi inspired me in so many ways. Mostly, she inspired me to pick up the ukulele and to start playing." This was just one of many messages that I received from Zoi's friends. And it's one of Zoi's many tracks that she imprinted upon us in her 15 years on this planet.

In the weeks after Zoi died, I learned a lot more about her than I thought I already knew, and I became even more proud of her. When she was in one of the hospital units, she would play her ukulele and sing to some of the kids. Often, it was the last thing the unit heard before they shut off the lights at night. I also learned that she would often attempt to translate what the counselors or staff would be saying to the other kids in their effort to help, and offer her own interpretation to her friends as a way to help them understand what they were both hearing and going through.

Zoi is a beautiful old soul. If you knew her personally, and if she made a connection with you, it was because you opened up to her and that was the depth that she wanted to live in. Zoi shared and gave all of herself to the kids at the hospital units, as well as to her family and her friends. To me, she did more at 15 years old than a lot of people have done by 90.

Several of her friends would tell me that Zoi was the first person to greet them when they came in to an adolescent unit. She would see how scared, tired and lost they were. And since she had been in that place of being emotionally drained, she could recognize and guide them right away by saying, "Hi, I'm Zoi. You got this." Or, "It's OK, it's not that bad and you're going to be OK." Instant connection and relationship.

When I think about these tracks that Zoi left, I know they will be remembered for many years to come, and by sharing them with you, for generations to come. I know that at the very least, the lessons and tracks she left us will stay with our family and all of her friends until the end of our days. Our tracks are our legacy that we impart in this world, and that last well after we have left this earth. I even listed some of the tracks I hope to leave, such as:

- He did so much for others in healing.
- He helped many people to overcome loss.
- He was a light and hope for people through the fog of loss.
- He recognized the capacity in all of us to heal.

I would like you to take a few moments to do this exercise for yourself. It will be a very revealing exercise and it will open your mind to your greater purpose. Grab a pen and/or a notebook, and find a quiet spot in your home. Give yourself about 10 to 15 minutes to work through this.

Before you start, take a few deep breaths and think about the person you would like to be there holding your hand as you take *your* last breath. Fifteen years pass, and that same person is sitting with someone having coffee. The other person asks about you and what you were like. What would you want the person who knew you to say about you? Those are the things that I would like you to write down. If you only have a few ideas, that's OK. You don't need to go into detail on these, just get it down on paper like I did with my examples above. Don't question what comes to your mind, just let it flow. This is for no one else except you.

Now take a few minutes to read those out loud to yourself. Yes, it will seem awkward. And yes, this was not an easy thing to do. It feels kind of strange to talk about yourself in this light, right? Well, this is why the exercise is for you and you alone. Doing this will help you to determine *your purpose* in this world. What is the common theme of your tracks?

31

A path emerges — framing your mindset

Back in 2005, I was seeking professional help. I had lost myself completely in my marriage to Maria and I wanted to better myself, for the kids' sake as well as my own. As I was trying to navigate my separation, and the upcoming divorce, I had no idea what life would be like as a single parent. I wanted to find and reconnect to who I was as a man, a family member and especially as a father. I had just spent the last seven years raising three kids. The relationships with them were so important to me, and this transition was so stressful, that I had to seek professional help and guidance.

I contacted a few therapists and one called me back very quickly to just book an appointment. But before I saw her, I received a call from just one other therapist, Dr. Howes. I thanked Dr. Howes for calling and told her I had another therapist booked already. But instead of just hanging up, she took the time to ask me what was going on. I told her that my marriage was breaking down and that I wanted to understand what made me tick. She gave me some sage advice that day: "Eric, I hope that everything works out. And while you explore therapy, be very critical of yourself — not in the sense that you beat yourself up, but rather, be completely open and honest with who you are, otherwise therapy is not going to help." I was very grateful to hear those words.

A week later, I was sitting across from the therapist I booked time with first. I was upset, I *was* being completely open and honest, and I was looking for some guidance and relief. At the 50-minute mark she promptly stopped me and said, "Our time is up, and I can't help you with what you are going through." I know she gave me some other referrals, and I thanked her for her time and just left. Remembering my conversation with Dr. Howes, I called her right away to see if she still had any availability. Luckily, she did and a week later, sitting across from her, I was upset, being completely open and honest, and looking for some guidance and relief. At the 50-minute mark, she stopped me and said, "Our time is up. So, what do you want to work on first, Eric?"

Deep breath.

That very next session we got to work. It was going to be a challenge though, because I was simultaneously stuck in the vacuum of the separation, I was questioning my capacity as a father, and I had no idea what to do to navigate a separation. I didn't have many coping skills. I mean, I could function and handle some areas of my life, like work, but mostly I was depressed and I didn't want to do anything with anyone. My best friend was isolation and I didn't think I had the strength to fight to feel better, ever. And that showed to all my family and friends.

Months went by, I had many sessions with Dr. Howes. She never did any of the work for me. She just gave me some nuggets to take with me and to process until our next session together. Over time, my internal strength built up, the depression eased and I felt like I could smile again, authentically. I got out more, I started to date and I did creative things like doing crafts, taking day trips to Salem, Massachusetts and traveling out of state with Zoi and Arminda. When struggles arose — and they always do, inside of any household — instead of reacting, I was responding. Instead of getting depressed, I was able to sort through my emotions and carry on. Instead of getting knocked down, I was able to take the "hit" and keep going.

When Zoi died, Dr. Howes graciously moved around her schedule to see me, and I was grateful for that. I remember early on in these therapy sessions, we were talking about how things had been after my marriage ended and what was the possibility of me being depressed again. I told her that while I feared that I would fall back into a deep hole of depression because of losing Zoi, I envisioned that hole to be the size of an ant hole. I couldn't fit in it, so I wasn't going to go there. That mindset helped me to stay upright through most of this process.

Often, when we suffer the loss of a loved one, we feel that we have to remain guilty and punish ourselves for the loss. I certainly did that too. But what I found was that when I reframed my mind from asking the question of "Why did this happen TO me?" to a new mindset of "Why is this happening FOR me?", a different path emerged. A path of opportunity, of light, and now a greater purpose.

I had to live into forgiveness for what I perceived I didn't do for Zoi. I had to forgive others around me whom I felt let me down with their actions after Zoi died. I had to forgive myself. But more important, when I accepted "what was" I began to feel grateful for not only being Zoi's father and having her in my life for 15 years, and I was grateful for everything else in my life. This was happening *for* me to step into a greater purpose that was much bigger than me. Expressing gratitude is huge positive disruptor on our journey through grief.

Reframing "How could you leave me?" or "How could you leave me and the kids like this?" also falls into this mindset shift. Let's look at this from the other perspective. About a year after Zoi died, I was at the cemetery visiting Zoi's resting place and met a woman whose husband took his life around the same time that Zoi took hers. No one in her family saw it coming, yet she was left with two stinging questions. One, "Why did he leave us like this?" And two, "What was wrong with me that he didn't talk to me about what he was going through?" Sharing my experience with losing Zoi, I offered this woman a different perspective on a suicide. That when someone takes their life, it's not to hurt us, and they don't necessarily want to end their life, but rather they want to end their pain. To us, there is no burden of their presence when they are alive. The family and also the world are *not* better off without them here. This is where forgiveness comes into play, and making peace with the loss so that gratitude replaces the grief. Second, there was nothing wrong with her as a person. They shared

126

23 years of marriage together and this was something that he had been battling all along. It wasn't about her.

I often see this woman at the cemetery and we usually hug and check in on each other. We're in this together and we'll get through this together too.

32

Functioning with intention

As I began to come out of the fog of losing Zoi, I started to live more intentionally and to believe that it was OK to do so. I had to give myself permission to be OK with 'going and doing' again and to be mindful that I would feel guilty at times. When I would feel guilt, I would remind myself that Zoi would want me to be happy no matter what I was doing.

Coming out of the fog is not the same experience for each of us. I can appreciate that you are all grieving and that you are at various stages of your grieving process. All I know is that as we walk through grief, we all have the capacity to come out of the fog. There is no timeline for that process, and everything we need to come out of the fog is already inside of us.

When we lose someone that we love, sometimes the things that used to make us feel really good may not feel good anymore, right? We feel no purpose, and as meaning-seeking, purpose-driven beings, that doesn't jive with how we feel in grief. Death can take our loved one's life, but it doesn't have to take ours. Getting on that path to feeling better *only* emerges when we start to do the work, when we give ourselves permission to do so. The permission to be OK is OK! If you're trying to find your way through the fog, and are completely stuck, thinking that you're never going to feel better, to be OK, or know how to find your way, let's talk about some simple and easy things that we can do each day to help us to keep moving forward, to live intentionally.

First, I had to accept that it was OK to be keep going and to do the things that I liked doing. I didn't have to feel guilty for taking care of myself. It was OK to be happy. I didn't have to feel bad for smiling or laughing. It was OK to cry and let it out. I didn't have to feel wrong for being sad. All of this is part of the grieving process.

Second, I had to rediscover what I was passionate about. I used to love going to the beach with the girls, traveling with them, and taking care of myself physically. But that was taking on a new meaning in my grief. Before you lost your loved one, what did you like to do by yourself or together with them? What did you use to do with him or her that you cherished, and that gave both of you energy? When you were growing up, what did you love to do? Was it sports or did you have a hobby? Have you always wanted to write a book? Have you wanted to travel, or try that new skydiving adventure? Doing what we love to do creates new memories and it heals us — body, mind and soul.

Being out in nature and taking care of myself physically has given me purpose again. When I'm out in nature, it feels like a return to a connection to my 10-year-old self — I feel like I did when I wandered the paths around my house in Brunswick, Maine. It is feeling that adventure and connectedness again. Exercising was something that I enjoyed when Zoi was a young child, up until she died. And when Zoi died, I stopped for a while. I got back on a consistent exercise routine and it reminded me that I functioned better when I ate well and worked out.

I traveled some with the girls growing up. We went to New Orleans a few times, which created incredible memories that I will cherish forever. After Zoi died, it took a couple of years, but then I started to travel on my own again. So far, it's all been in the U.S., and I've seen some amazing things that I will take in with my two eyes and share with Zoi when we are reunited. I'm now planning to travel to Switzerland, France and Greece.

A new passion has been learning how to write and tell my story of Zoi, as it serves something bigger than me and helps others.

I also like to meditate often. It has reconnected me with Zoi and now I'm creating new memories of her. It's allowing me to function with the intention of living a fully life.

Four months after Zoi died, I was back part-time at work. After a really stressful day in the office, I left work that particular day feeling very frustrated and irritated. I was an exposed nerve in many ways. I asked my boss if I could leave a little early and headed for the train. I was expecting people to act differently, but people will continue to be the people they are regardless of the situation *you're* in. It's your job to become resilient like a tree that grows on a cliffside. The roots go deeper and the trunk gets stronger. I walked to the train station feeling completely pressurized from the day. I was feeling guilty, missing Zoi so much that I just needed to connect with her. I got on the train and I sat down. It was noisy between the sounds of the train and the fans circulating air in the railcar. I felt like I wanted to cry my eyes out. Why wasn't Zoi here any longer? The noise from the people talking around me and the creaking of the train going over the tracks were not helping. The acrid smell of the brakes was making me sick to my stomach.

I closed my eyes and said to myself, "Find the most peaceful place to be where you actually feel like there is no stress there." My mind's eye opened up to a high-elevation lake. The water there was so calm it looked like a sheet of glass, except for these tiny waves rolling up on the black onyx rock shoreline. Where I stood further up the beach, the sand hugged my feet. The sky: dusk, with deep blue, blending into the pink, blending into the yellow of the sunlight that was behind a mountain across the other side of the lake. Not a sound. Warm. I looked fully to my right, to my left, and up where the stars were starting to appear as the sun was setting. Behind me was a beach about 30 feet right at the base of another mountain. I just listened to the nothingness and felt at peace. I felt loved there. I could see it all and with such clarity and detail.

Then, Zoi approached me from the left. She was wearing a long, flowing dress. The dress was the same colors as the sky — deep blue, pink and yellow — all flowing together seamlessly. I felt her presence and I felt warm. The first thing I asked was, "Are you OK?" "Dad, I am *more* than OK." My heart warmed further. I asked her if she was a god. And she said no, but that she was now god-like. "I am guidance, but you, Dad, are light and hope." I asked more questions and each answer was more comforting than the last. I asked her about my life and what was coming — and she told me that things would get better. That I just have to keep going. I promised her that I would take care of the family and her friends, and she was happy about that. She told me that I should come to this place any time I want. That it will always be there for me to come back to, and that she would always be there too. We hugged.

I opened my eyes — it was 20 minutes later and I hadn't slept. All of the stress I had been feeling was washed away. I felt connected and like I had taken the longest swim in the most comfortable pool ever. I was so glad that I had that experience. The thing is, I had never been able to visually meditate before this.

In a February 9, 2015 Forbes.com article, Alice G. Walton notes that based on many recent studies, "The practice [of meditation] appears to have an amazing variety of neurological benefits…and helps relieve our subjective levels of anxiety and depression, and improve attention, concentration, and overall psychological well-being."

In a *Yale Scientific* article dated May 10, 2012 and titled "The Healing Art of Meditation," author Kaitlin McLean examines Dr. Judson Brewer's work at the Yale School of Medicine. Dr. Brewer has identified functional changes in the brain of experienced meditators using fMRI imaging in a study to show meditation's impact on the brain.

Dr. Brewer started meditating during medical school to reduce stress. He found it very helpful and 10 years later, he began to study it clinically using the noninvasive fMRI method, which measures oxygen levels in the brain. Dr. Brewer performed fMRI brain scans on both experienced mediators and inexperienced meditators, both at rest and while using mindfulness meditation — a type of meditation that encourages acute awareness of physical or spiritual realities. The subjects of the study used three types of mindfulness meditation techniques:

1. Concentration — the subject focuses on breathing.
2. Loving kindness — the subject focuses on a feeling of good toward oneself and others that is supported by silently repeating phrases such as "May X be happy."
3. Choiceless awareness — the subject can focus on whatever object comes to them.

Two notable trends emerged from Brewer's research. First, experienced meditators showed deactivation of the brain known as the default mode network (DMN) or "daydreaming" brain. Second, different networks of the brain were talking to each other, which had not been seen before in this context. Daydreaming, it seems, does not make us happier. It's a resistance system intended to keep us from the things that we should be doing. Therefore, reducing our daydreaming can affect our emotional health positively. And we do that by meditating. Mindfulness training can help anxiety, chronic pain, addictions and other disorders, but exactly how meditation affects these conditions is still unknown.

As Kaitlin McLean suggests at the end of her article, there are many ways to get introduced to meditation. For starters, *Mindfulness in Plain English* by Bhante Gunaratana is a book that you can download for free. There are also many mobile apps available that can help with guided meditations.

Last, and maybe you've heard of this as well, some schools are replacing detention with meditation. In a *U.S. News & World Report* article dated December 8, 2016, author Angela Haupt discovers an elementary school in Baltimore that has replaced detention with meditation. At Robert W. Coleman Elementary School, kids practice deep-breathing exercises, meditate and talk about what happened if they got into trouble. It's one example of how mindfulness is becoming a standard part of the school day, offering an alternative to the usual punishments and, advocates say, arming kids with lifelong tools to cope with challenging situations, resolve conflicts and feel compassion and empathy for both themselves and others.

Do you remember Anna's story from earlier? As a child that had to deal with the loss of her father from suicide, she has done a lot to ensure she is growing from her loss. She has a purpose and now owns her own hair salon. Owning became a passion for her after many years of "renting" a chair in another salon. Anna shared with me that when she was renting the chair at a previous salon, she faced many obstacles. For her, the chair rental in that salon was expensive, plus she had to use only the products the salon sold for her clients. And she had no key to the building. Everything was monitored. She felt like she was working for them even though she rented her own chair. As Anna put it, "I wasn't inspired. It was too much of a struggle for what I loved to do." No wonder she was questioning whether she wanted to continue as a stylist or to find another passion.

Now, as an entrepreneur and business owner, she has more clients, she's gaining more new clients, and she has much more freedom to function as she needs to. She has the key to the building and to her own shop. One of the more important discoveries is that her creativity has come alive. She now puts her energy and time into learning the art of retail and expanding her business. She says, "The law of attraction is in effect — when you're open to new energy, good energy is drawn to you. It's starting to get fun! I was 100 percent nervous, but also knew 100 percent it was the right thing to do to open my own salon. My faith was bigger than the fears."

So let me ask you, what fills you up to function with intention as you're coming out of the fog of grief?

33

My other family and a new direction

When Zoi died, I let myself go physically. The wakeup call for me was when I had lower back pain and soreness getting out of bed, low energy, and wasn't eating optimally (or at least within healthy parameters for my body). For most of us, a poor state of health creeps up on us. And in the midst of grief, it is more likely that we'll turn to our "comfortable" habits or vices that weren't serving us very well to begin with. Some of these even become accelerated.

We think that our bodies can function indefinitely — doing the things that we did when we were younger. And for those of you who *are* younger, changing these habits *now* can and will affect your future self in so many ways. Not only do we benefit physically, but physical activity is the least expensive antidepressant on the market, and one of the most effective methods to getting your body and mind aligned and feeling better.

When I started to exercise again, I had to give myself permission that it was going to be awhile before I felt healthy. I didn't need to start up at 100 mph, I just needed to start. At first, I struggled to get most of the exercise reps in and found myself struggling even more to keep up with even modified moves. I was shaking off months of rust and I had to ramp up again at my pace.

As a Beachbody coach, traveling to the annual coach summit events was both good and awkward. After Zoi died, I was conflicted on whether I should even go or not. Going would be good in the sense that I would reconnect with many of my fellow coach friends, who are like a second family to me. But it would be awkward too, because I struggled with how my coaching business was not growing. I was comparing myself to other coaches who started after me and who were doing really well in the business in a shorter period of time. It took some time to stop comparing myself to anyone else. I had my path and they had theirs. Just like with this journey of grief, we are all doing our own thing. No one can walk the path for us and each of us has to do our own work.

After the Beachbody Summit, several months passed before I saw an invite on Facebook for a Men's Leadership event in Dallas, Texas. I signed up right away. I was amped about reenergizing my focus on what we as men are capable of doing in this business. At this event, we were introduced to Bo Eason — he was going to show us the impact of storytelling in our businesses. I only knew about Bo's brother, Tony, who was the quarterback of the New England Patriots between 1983 and 1989, and led them to their first-ever Super Bowl in 1985 against the Chicago Bears. Bo, also a former NFL player, had transitioned to storytelling after writing and performing a semi-autographical play on Broadway for 10 years.

"When I was 9 years old, I had a plan to become the best safety in the NFL." This was Bo's opening sentence for us, and we were hooked. I couldn't look away and I wanted to know more. Bo told us the story of his freshman year of college, when he was trying to get on the football team at UC Davis. Conflict after conflict came up along his journey, but he didn't quit, until the final game of the season, where he created an opportunity that changed his life and direction forever. As Bo was going through his story, I located myself in it as well. I began to think of my early struggles in life. His story connected to my heart and head. You see, that is the power of story. As humans we are biologically wired to connect through story.

Bo then offered us the chance to come work with him. My heart lit up, and I threw caution to the wind. I was going to tell the world about Zoi!

34

When my beautiful daughter Zoi...

A few months after the event in Dallas and signing up with Bo, I landed in San Diego for his event. It was beautiful in La Jolla, California. The weather was unreal, 75 degrees and sunny. The room at the hotel was one of the smallest I'd ever stayed in, but still awesome. I was grateful to be there. The next morning, we piled into the theatre and took our seats.

Bo came out and immediately had us dialed in with another story. He told us that most likely no one else had ever given us permission to be the best, but things would be different here. And if we wanted to be players, not spectators, we were welcome to stay. No amateurs were allowed. We got to work and we learned about personal story, our personal story. Also, the story that we didn't want to tell was the one that we should tell here. It was a defining moment in our lives.

I knew before coming to La Jolla that I wanted to talk about Zoi, but resistance kicked in. As we started to write our own story, I went with some benign story about when I was in sixth grade, and the girl that I had a huge crush on sat next to me at lunch one day. I couldn't believe it… my dream girl sitting right in front of me. I tried to act cool and didn't say much. I pulled out a Devil Dog and she snatched it from the table and squished it. I told on her. Yep, I told on her and didn't waste a second in doing so. This was truly an awkward teen moment. I don't know why I chose that as my defining moment over telling Zoi's story.

"Tim, I don't think I like my story." These are the first words I said to story coach Tim Dixon as we ended our first day of the event. Tim asked, "Tell me what you have." "Well, I was in sixth grade and I was crushing on a girl and she sat next to me at lunch one day. I took out a Devil Dog, she squished it in her hands and I told on her." Tim looked at me. "OK, what else you got?" "Well, I lost my daughter Zoi to suicide about two years ago?" Tim's eyes got wide and he said, "My heart just sank when you told me that. THAT is your story!" I left with a new purpose.

A new friend and I went to dinner and my mind was spinning. I didn't know where to begin with this story, but I had a good idea. After dinner, I went back to my hotel and crashed at 9 p.m. My body clock was still on East Coast time anyway. I woke up at midnight tossing and turning. I was going over this story over and over. I turned on the light in the room, grabbed my notebook and started writing for the next two hours. I started my story the moment that I walked into the ER that night expecting to hear that Zoi was breathing again. I wrote about 20 pages and recalled some pretty difficult details. I cried so much that night, yet it was cathartic. I hadn't gone into that much detail since Zoi had died 21 months earlier.

I woke up the next day feeling rested and ready to go in this new direction. On the Day 2 agenda: Physicality and how that affects our stage presence — how we connect to the audience in front of us. Body language, being open, not apologizing for who we are as men or women, the predatory nature that we all have inside of us. During an exercise with movement coach Jean-Louis Rodrigue, we were to connect via meditation with an ancestor. I invited Zoi to come into my body. As we went deeper into the meditation I felt a strange sensation, like I was starting to breathe again — as if Zoi was taking breaths again. I could see in my mind's eye that she was radiant, with longer wavy blond hair. She was adorned with beautiful jewelry — a very delicate pearl and gold necklace — and she wore a blue dress. We talked for a little bit and then we had to let go of that person, releasing them. I watched Zoi walk back into the light and she waved to me.

Day 3 arrived, and we talked about generosity and how that isn't anything about giving money, but rather giving ALL of yourself to whatever it is that you are doing for others, especially on the stage. Later in the day we spent more time opening up and telling our stories again. This time, I felt better knowing that my story was going to come out as it should be coming out. I walked up to the front of the stage, took a deep breath and said, "When my beautiful daughter Zoi took her life 21 months ago..." and I paused because I almost forgot the rest, "...I didn't know what I was going to do, but all I did know was that I was going to fight for my family and all of Zoi's friends to find the pathway back to better days." It felt like that pause between my sentence and Bo's coaching lasted forever. Bo invited me down to the bottom of the stage. He could barely talk. He said that he didn't know how I was still standing, and as a father himself, that he might not ever be able to get back up if something like that happened to him.

Before we left that last day, Bo made yet another offer to work with him further in his Mastermind group, and I accepted that offer as well. This weekend absolutely showed me that I was being called to something bigger than me. That I had to help Zoi's friends and even kids/parents that I didn't know yet to get back to better days. It was a new journey I was being called to action on.

35

Formation of core values.

What are your core values? What is it that brings energy and direction to your life? When thinking about your core values, they dictate your behavior and action. When I met Bo Eason, my life was dramatically changed after he told only one story — and it had nothing to do with business or money. It was his personal story about when he was 9 years old and dreamed of playing pro football. He was literally and figuratively "the runt of the litter" and had to work even harder toward his goal of becoming a pro football player. Bo never gave up, he worked every single day, and with the formation of his core values, he practiced every single day. He dedicated himself to the problem of being small and fought against the resistance of doing nothing about it. He did all of this until he reached his goal and was drafted as a top safety pick in the 1984 NFL draft. When Bo made me the offer to work with him, I jumped! I had permission to tell my story in the hopes of helping others overcome loss. I had energy and direction pouring out of me.

A close friend of mine, Leslie Harrington, talks about her life's direction after moving through many losses in life. "My youngest impactful experience was when I was 16. We just got the call that my 26-year-old half-brother Steve had taken his life. The doctors blamed it on the meds, but it didn't add up. Steve lived with his mom and my dad was left in the dark on the details of my brother's bipolar diagnosis and prior attempts at suicide, so the call was quite shocking. I had a lot of questions and struggled, so I immersed myself in suicide support groups, psychology classes, and most importantly, I researched medications. When the doctors blamed the suicide on the meds, I had to know why. What didn't make sense was that Steve had a lot of good things going for him — he was engaged to be married, and he had just started a successful business with my other half-brother, Bruce. There were a lot of misconceptions around him taking his life." Leslie felt that seeing the pain her family was in, was so hard to accept. She struggled to understand how medications as well as Steve's "depth of pain" could have caused him to make a decision to end his life.

After high school, Leslie studied at the local community college to be close to her first love, Dustin, who was a year younger than her. Shortly after the first semester started, Leslie was faced with yet another loss — Dustin was killed in a car accident. "When he died, the emotions were drastically different than my brother's death in two ways. First, the relationships and interactions were different between my older brother and my boyfriend." And second, the intimacy she shared with her boyfriend made this loss very different. Leslie was distraught in the days after the loss of Dustin. So much so that her parents took her to an emergency crisis clinic, where she met with a counselor who drilled her with questions about suicide. She laments that while she was experiencing a lot of grief and sadness, "I was in no way wanting to hurt myself. I was just really sad. My dad was having a tough time with my being sad, though. It was really my mom that was my rock. She was a 'get it out' type of person. And Dad was a 'keep it all in' kind of guy. But I just needed to be sad and get through it. My resilience didn't start then — I just went through the motions to survive and get through the days."

Leslie says she shut down for a while. "When you are 18, and it's your first love, you think it's the best thing ever, the greatest love. It's such a pure, fearless love because you haven't been hurt or become guarded." It took Leslie some time to get back into her college classes, eventually earning her undergraduate degree from FSU and graduate degree in psychology at Nova Southeastern University, where her father, Bill, was a professor. She dated again, but always kept the boys at arm's length. "I was reluctant to love out of fear of losing them. I never really had a strong connection. I eventually had to let go of being unlovable."

About four years ago Leslie received some news that her mother, Laurice, had been diagnosed with cancer. It was an aggressive form of bladder cancer. After battling through chemo, the results were in. The cancer had spread and her mother's best chances for life expectancy was six months to a year. "I had 'fall to your knees crying' moments."

But, she approached her mom's diagnosis with a "Let's crush this" mentality. She did research, and she planned and worked with the doctors to do everything she could to help her mom get through it. But life had other plans. Despite starting treatments right away, just six weeks after the prognosis, Leslie lost her best friend and confidant, her mom.

When it comes to living your life, you always have an alternative way of looking and approaching your options as both positive and negative thoughts naturally flow through your mind. Leslie wasn't sure what direction she was going to go in: a long period of sadness or grief, or the *direction of love*. She chose the energy and direction of love. In her words, "Who was despondence going to serve?" In her mind, going toward the easily accessed negativity was always worse than fighting for the difficult positivity she needed.

Leslie sought the help of her therapist right away. She knew she had to talk to someone because she would shut down if she didn't. She began to uncover how connected to spirituality she was. She didn't fully understand why her mom had to go, but as that was her mom's journey, this was her journey. She wasn't mad at God for what had happened. Life took on a new meaning for her: she connected to new things and different people. Tolerance for any bullshit went right out the door.

Her newfound sensitivity to toxic energy gave her the push to seek out quality relationships with new people. When the negativity was removed from her life, she found that she began to attract Laurice-like people into her life. She decided to end her 15-year career in pharmaceuticals. Her days were then *built by her design*, rather than following someone else's plan for her. Leslie learned to put her energy where it would be the most useful — outward, toward others.

Good energy is like an untapped river. Leslie took the time for what really mattered in her life. She learned about energy. She learned that when you have hyperventilating moments and feel like you can't take another step forward, use that *good* energy and put it in the best places possible. For her, it was three main things:

1. Surround yourself with amazing people, and form positive new relationships with those who see greatness in you.
2. Life HAS to go on. When the dust settles, you still have to put one foot in front of the other. Sometimes, you have to fake it until you make it. Act as if…
3. Live in love, not fear. We owe it to ourselves and our loved ones to shift our energy outward by focusing on how we can help and serve others.

About two years after her mom died, Leslie had a major breakthrough that came in the form of guided meditation, where she felt fully connected with her mother's soul. From that moment on, she knew her mom was still her guiding light. "If your mind is full of junk, you can't make room for the right energy to come in." She also knew that she had to help herself before she could help anyone else.

Anna recently ran her first Spartan race. She was nervous about this race. She never felt like quitting practice, but rather, she wanted to exceed her own expectations when it came time to run the race. She focused on three things that gave her energy and direction:

1. The goal of finishing the race.

2. The outcome — how she would feel crossing the finish line.
3. The physical obstacles, and how she would approach and overcome them.

"For me, finishing the race equated to life itself — I knew I could conquer it and keep going," says Anna. "At one of the obstacles, it required us to climb over a tall wooden wall. I fell off the first couple of times. I got back up again and climbed on a guy's shoulders and expected someone to catch me on the other side, but I landed by myself. I knew my dad would be proud of me for that."

When we have energy and direction in life, we lead more purposeful, meaningful and happier lives. We thrive! Moving toward these better days is a journey and not a destination, just as life itself is. Living a life where you thrive and grow when the sun is shining prepares you for when the storm clouds come, and they will.

In the last section of this book, we'll look at what thriving in life feels like. I'll share some of the experiences that I've had along my journey. We'll go deeper into how to stay in that world of resilience and to make this your constant for the rest of your life.

PART IV

THRIVING

"Search your heart and see. The way to do is to be."

— Lao Tzu

36

Why should I thrive?

"I'm surviving and I'm perfectly fine with that." This was the response from Donna in a grief and loss Facebook group not very long ago. Donna had experienced the sudden loss of her husband of 34 years to a heart attack. It was all that she could do to get out of bed each morning. When I read that, it brought me back to when I was mourning Zoi. There were days when I didn't want to get out of bed at all.

When I asked Donna what it would take for her to feel like she had consistently better days, to where she would be thriving, she hadn't given it much thought. She had been stuck, and felt that if she could survive the loss of her husband, she would be OK with that. In talking with her further, she really didn't want to be just surviving. She shared that thriving again meant to her that she had a purpose, and that resilience was more prevalent in her life than the sadness of losing her husband. She just didn't know how to move past grief.

The definition of resilience is the capacity to cope with, adjust, or recover from stress or adversity. It is also the process and outcome of successfully adapting to difficult or challenging life experiences and to rise above one's circumstances. I'm expanding on the definition of resilience: true resilience is the capacity to withstand adversity, surpass mere survival and thrive.

Leslie Harrington talks about how when you experience loss, you are put on a path of either remaining stuck in survival mode or you move toward a path of resilience, growth and thriving. She defined it as the direction of love. "Sometimes, we do survive by instinct. But that is only temporary. People say, I don't know how you do it. It's not how I do it, it's that I just do it. You don't know what you can do until the time comes. Sometimes, strength is all you have, and it will be enough to get you through the worst of it." She now thrives on creating new ways to help people lead a healthy way of life, free of manufactured medications.

Leslie's specific advice to thrive:

- See the positive, cool things that are going on around you.
- Journal the positivity.
- Develop gratitude.

Anna credits her preparation for her Spartan races as her acceptance of thriving. She knew it was going to be hard work, and that she had to employ regimen, ritual and rigor at each practice. The regimen was the training of obstacles each day. The ritual was doing it every day. And the rigor was how intensely she practiced each day. In her words, "It was empowering and exciting!" I asked some additional questions of Anna recently:

- *What were some of the things that happened along the way that made you stronger?* "Contrasting life and the Spartan race; I may fall down, but I get back up and keep going. When you know you can and then believe you can do something, then you are unstoppable!"

- *If you had to go back in time to say anything to your 5-year-old self when you learned your dad died, what would you say to that 5-year-old Anna?* "You are going to do things you never thought were possible. And, we're going to have a conversation one day about losing our dad. I'm going to tell you that you're going to make something of yourself. It's ALL going to stem from this moment, right now."

- *What about your 14-year-old self? What would you tell Anna, even if your father were alive?* "You're still going to have doubts, you'll still stumble and fall. You'll get hurt. Life can be shitty, and messed-up things are going to happen. You're going to make mistakes. You're going to have to live through it, though. With all of these things happening, you are going to blame it on that fact that your father took his life as being the root cause. But all of those decisions — you have to own them. The choice he made was all his. It had nothing to do with you. So, take ownership of your life. Grow, and listen to the people around you."

- When you are in the middle of grief, your focus is on survival, first. It's also that losing someone you love just *sucks*, and you don't want to feel this way at all! It's a focus on the questions that we ask ourselves, and on the amount of time that it takes to navigate grief. My resilience was built on:
- Answering my questions one by one, and accepting the discovered truth of each answer.
- *Framing* my mindset differently and making peace with what was, so that I could become grateful for what is.
- *Functioning* with intention on what made my heart sing: traveling, meditations, story work, leadership. It meant getting my feet on the ground each morning and taking care of myself through exercise, and focusing on others.
- *Formation* of my core values. Being called to do something that was bigger than I am gave my life so much energy and direction — a greater purpose!

37

I find my tribe

When I enrolled in Bo Eason's Mastermind group, it afforded me the opportunity to take my story and get even more specific with it. However, before the Mastermind group met in L.A. for the first time, we were provided a couple of sessions with the wonderful story coach on Bo's staff, Mary Kincaid. Mary's goal is to help you find the meat of your story. After my sessions with Mary, I had a good foundation for how my story was to be structured. It felt great to be getting closer, but I also knew that I had much more work to do.

In late January 2016, I arrived in L.A. for the first Mastermind session. For two days, we worked on opening up to express ourselves physically, so that when it came time to tell our story on a stage, we would be prepared. Immediately, I knew this was the right place to be. I had never been connected to so many people standing shoulder to shoulder, always supporting each other as we fought to bring our message to the world through our story. I was with my tribe. As humans, we are wired to connect with a tribe, but more importantly, we are wired to connect via story. It heals the brain. It breeds trust, reciprocity, hospitality and empathy in all of us. Languages have been around for about 10,000 years, but story itself has been used long before that, in cave paintings and other forms of body language and gestures. We see and read body language before a word is ever muttered out of someone's mouth. And, when you have a collective group of people standing shoulder to shoulder, fighting for your dreams as you are for theirs, you are with your tribe.

38

A class of 300

I was reluctant to make the call to Zoi's school. What was I about to commit to? Would they even go for what I was going to ask them?

Through a series of calls, I finally got ahold of Jon, the principal. Jon was new to the high school that year. He had heard of Zoi through other teachers and administrators. We talked a bit and I asked point blank if I could speak at this graduation ceremony, as it would have been Zoi's class. My message would be relevant to not only the kids, but also the parents. Jon had to decline the actual graduation, but instead offered for me to come speak to the senior class at a pre-graduation event at the school. I got choked up and was grateful to have this first opportunity to speak. While I knew a lot of the kids that Zoi grew up with, it had been many years since I'd seen most of them. Some knew me only as Zoi's dad, and others were closer to me because of their relationship to Zoi.

On the day of the event, I met Jon in the lobby to shake his hand.

He showed me the auditorium and said that he would be introducing me before the day of events got started. As the kids started to come into the auditorium, some who knew me ran up and hugged me. They asked me what I was doing there and I told them it was a surprise.

The kids took their seats and Jon introduced me. I shared the story of how we named Zoi, like you read earlier in the book. Afterward, I asked if it would be OK if I shared three things about living their lives in case we never saw each other again. They gladly accepted this offer. Here's what I shared with them:

1. Live your life and be passionate about it.

A former high school classmate of mine, Roby, is a world traveler. When I tell you he is like the real-life version of the Dos Equis guy, I'm not kidding. He travels all over the world, it seems everyone knows him, he enjoys meeting new people, and loves living life. Every month Roby is off again on another trip or adventure: BOOM, GONE! And a lot of these trips are at locations you usually only see in movies. He immerses himself in the experience to take it all in.

Most people don't know this, but Roby works from 7 a.m. to 11 p.m. most days. You see my friends, the dream is free, but the journey is not. When you do find that thing you are passionate about, and some of you already have, you will never be disappointed by that decision, ever. There will be days when it will be great, and there's going to be days when it will suck. Embrace the suck — it's part of the process. Those struggles and failures prepare you for the success later on. You may want to give up and quit when things aren't going well, and most people do. But that's when you dig in, play a bigger game and work harder. Because success and the life you want to lead are on the other side of that hard work. The dreams you have today mean something to you, and it will mean the world to you when you achieve them. Don't ever give up on that passion, and live LIFE!

2. Generosity — give all of yourself in what you do.

When most people think of generosity, they think of someone giving them some money. I'm not talking about that type of generosity. I'm talking about giving all of yourself in what you do.

Zoi received a ukulele on her thirteenth birthday. Actually, she took the $100 she got from her grandmother for school clothes and bought the ukulele because she wanted it so bad. And in a very short period of time, she learned a tremendous amount of chords and played some of her favorite songs, from Nirvana to the Red Hot Chili Peppers.

When she played and sang, it lifted her up. She often took the opportunity to play for others: especially she played and sang for her new friends when they were feeling down, even if she herself wasn't at 100 percent. After Zoi died, many of her new friends and even some adults wrote us, telling us how much Zoi influenced them to pick up and start learning the ukulele. Zoi saw music as her connective tissue with others. What it comes down to is that the really good gifts in life aren't wrapped in paper and don't come in monetary value, but rather the best gifts are wrapped in attention, connection and the value you give generously to others around you.

3. When you fall seven times, always get up eight times.

Last year, I had the honor of meeting Billy McDonald. Billy was stabbed twice, once at 11 and at 13 years old, but learned how to defend himself. He was in 11 school systems in between first grade and 12th. He was kicked out of his house at 16, but graduated near the top of his high school class. Billy went on to serve two decades in the United States Army Special Forces as a Green Beret. Just a couple of years ago, Billy lost most of the use of right arm after a gym accident, yet he has fought to regain as much use of his arm as possible, and to this day he continues to get back up — always one more time than he gets knocked down.

After Zoi died, it took months before I started to feel somewhat normal. I was eating like crap, I stopped exercising. My head just wasn't in the right place and I let myself go. And it took a lot of time for it to sink in that Zoi would be so frigging pissed off at me if she knew I was letting all of these good memories from her past stop my life from moving forward. She would be kicking my ass! And let me tell you, you don't want to piss off a Greek woman. But I stood back up because I knew that I had a greater purpose — to help not only myself but also my family and all of Zoi's friends find a pathway to better days.

I am so very proud of each and every one of you. You have worked hard and earned something that can never be taken away from you. This is not a participation award — your diploma is a representation of your hard work to get to this point today. You are the best. Go, live your life, find your passion and do it! Give ALL of yourself. And when life knocks you down, you get back up and kick its ass!

It was a true honor to speak on that stage that day. To see these kids whom Zoi knew so well and to connect with them. I feel as though I adopted 300 kids and became their dad as well.

39

Graduation Day meditation

I woke up on the Saturday of the graduation, just a few days after I had spoken to Zoi's class. I spent the morning trying to distract myself. On Facebook, I started to see pics of Zoi's classmates and friends in their caps and gowns, and it hit even harder. I was fantasizing that Zoi was standing there with them and how it would have felt to be there with her on that day. It brought me back to the very first day of school for Zoi. I still have a few photos from that day of me walking in with Zoi, hand in hand.

I went up into Zoi's room and sat on her bed in a mess of tears. Even though it had been two-and-a-half years since she died, I was found myself seriously wondering how it was possible that she was not there right now. I started to think more about the pictures that would've been taken that day, her laughing with her friends, and our family cheering her as she got her diploma. But all of that fantasizing just made it worse.

Sobbing, I thought of that peaceful place that she said I could always go to, the high-elevation lake, and I was back there instantly. Only this time, as I was standing on the shoreline of the lake, I heard something behind me that sounded like a small crowd. As I turned, I could see a circus-like tent behind me on the beach. The tent was about 6'x6' and about 10' tall. Blue and white vertical stripes, with a red flag at the top. I walked up the beach, still sobbing, and opened the flap to go in. Almost immediately, Zoi came right up to me. She grabbed my arms, looked me in the eyes and said, "Dad, stop… you can't come in here like this." Behind Zoi was a much larger space inside of the tent. There were several round picnic-like tables set up with a white candle centerpiece with white flowers at the base. There were a lot of people in there that I didn't recognize at all. Some were talking in Greek and others in English, yet everyone could understand each other. It then dawned on me that these were relatives from both my side of the family and her mother's who have died. They were there celebrating Zoi's graduation for her on that day. I looked back at Zoi, told her that I was so very proud of her. My tears stopped and I came out of the meditation. The rest of that day was OK. In fact, some of Zoi's classmates were posting that they knew she was with them in spirit that day. It warmed my heart and made me smile.

40

Spartans rising

In late September 2016, I attended the Spartans Rising Leadership Event in Tampa led by Scott Mann. For two days we learned some of the same lessons that Scott teaches new Green Berets on how to lead from the bottom up in a trust-depleted society, how to connect deeply to others with your story, and ultimately, how to determine our tracks for living into our greater purpose.

This training spoke to my soul and it connected me to my roots of growing up in Maine. It showed me how trust gaps are present in our society but can be bridged in families, communities and as a nation. It made me aware of what gaps are in my family that need to be bridged.

And all of this leadership starts with us stepping into the arena, getting scuffed up and immersing ourselves inside of the problem. No one else is coming to solve the problem for us. We need to to lead from the bottom up and go up on the "rooftop." Rooftop leadership is a specialized set of skills that allows you to make an impact with purpose that is much bigger than you are. And it inspires others to follow you, not because they have to, but because they choose to. We all have the capacity to lead ourselves first, then our families, our community, our nation and the world. There is no leadership out there that can do for our lives what we can ultimately do for ourselves. Everything we need is inside of us. When the training ended, Scott offered to work more closely with us to become better rooftop leaders, and I jumped at the opportunity to become a pathfinder.

One of the best components of this smaller pathfinder group was the specialized training that we would be getting from Scott directly. One of the very first events was participating in a Green Beret–style immersion to reconnect with nature, our nature, and get clear on our purpose for the impact we want to make. Knowing that Scott had led many successful operations in the military, I wanted to learn and go deep into my tracks with this leadership model.

In mid January 2017, I flew to Tampa, Florida for my immersion. Scott instructed me and my teammate John to stay at a local hotel and he would pick us up at 0700 hours.

When Scott showed up at the hotel, we wasted no time in getting on the road. Well outside of the Tampa city limits we pulled over off Highway 39 and turned onto this unassuming dirt road. The sign on the gate read:

Shoot Shack Gun Range

and Archery Club

We bounced along a long dirt road in Scott's older Chevy Suburban with 220,000 miles on it. Scott told us about this farmland on the way in, and how Gary and his family were like a clan of their own. Gary's house and the Shoot Shack came into view. We saw two guys working on a particular truck, which was one of about 20 vehicles strewn around the property in various phases of disrepair. The property didn't look so much like a junkyard as it did as a project workspace for their creations. We stopped, got out and the two men looked up at us. Scott said a few words to the two guys and they acknowledged him. John and I were ignored, untrusted.

Scott told us a little bit about what we should expect for the next 36 hours. He gave us the rundown of what was in our rucksacks. These were backpacks with all of the essentials and tools needed for this immersion. He showed us the gun range where we'd spend the afternoon of the first day. He asked us to take in what we were seeing — the lay of the land, the sights and sounds, the environment, all of it. He then pointed off into the direction of some wooded areas and said that was our destination. We left the car where it was, and we started on our way.

We approached John's campsite first and Scott gave him specific instructions. He told John to make the area his own. "Before you start, take five minutes and do your SLLS. Get yourself situated and we'll reconvene in one hour and start our day." SLLS is short for Stop, Look, Listen and Smell. This was something that 12-man Special Forces teams do the second they land on new territory during a mission. It provides your senses with additional input of the surroundings. If something isn't right, one of your senses will pick that up. Scott and I then moved off and approached my campsite, which was about 50 yards away from John's. Scott provided similar instructions for me and I got to work.

My campsite was underneath a few very old oak trees, with Spanish moss weeping down from the branches. A dead palm tree lay about three meters from where I was setting up. I used my feet to clear the ground beneath me of leaves, twigs and other incendiary materials, and I started collecting some sticks from around the area for my fire. The dead palm fronds were going to provide some excellent materials for my campfire.

I built my hooch — a makeshift, low-to-the-ground shelter — using the tarp supported with parachute string tied between an elderly strong oak with a twisted base and a smaller tree just 10 feet away. An old tractor wheel and some bungie cords provided the necessary support for this makeshift sleeping surface. I started my fire with the mag bar and flint, and was amped to be ready for the day ahead of us.

A short while later, after setting up his own site 100 yards downrange from John and me, Scott came up to my site, took pictures and asked how I was doing. He and I talked about clarity — for my intention of what I wanted to get out of this immersion experience, what I wanted to be clear on with my tracks and my story, and what my vision was for a tomorrow that didn't exist yet but that we need to discover. In other words, what would it take to fulfill my greater purpose of helping others overcome loss and thrive in life. It was emotional talking to him about this because of everything that had taken place over the previous three years that led up to me being on this 400-acre farm with him and John. Being outside in this environment was new to John, and it reminded me of being in the woods in Maine when I was 10 years old.

As part of this immersion experience, John and I took part in a four-hour weapons training session. I now have greater appreciation that we as humans we are at the top of the food chain for a reason. One, because we have the capacity to be lethal if we need to be. And two, that we are meaning-seeking, purpose-driven beings. Combined, both create the capacity for us to rise above baser instincts and thrive in life. We haven't spent the last million years being prey. We have the capacity to protect our family and the clan. We can provide food and shelter. We can respect life and its fragility. What an eye-opener! As the session went on, John and I learned proper weapons handling, how to respond to active shooter situations, how to provide immediate medical care to anyone that is wounded, and how to move on targets if we ever have a weapon in hand. Walking away from this training gave John and I had a deeper sense of connectedness to our nature.

Later, dinner around the campfire was a unique experience. In this primal setting you don't care if a food is prepared a certain way or how it comes to you, you accept the environment you're in and eat what is provided. Scott started off by cooking up some onions. And then he cooked up burgers on his campfire, which we all ate heartily. With the crackle of the fire and the smell of burgers and onions hanging in the air, we shared stories for several hours. Some of the stories were funny, some were downright serious, some were hard to hear — but altogether they created a deeper connection between all three of us. It was getting late and we had more work to do in the morning.

John and I retired to our respective campsites, headlamps illuminating the ground ahead of us. Crickets and unusual animal sounds were coming from all directions. Man, that SLLS really dials you in to your environment. Although our bodies began to adapt to being outside, it was getting colder as the night pressed on. I needed to get my fire going again. I walked the perimeter of my encampment and gathered more burning materials. The dead palm fronds were plentiful, but they burned easily, and quickly. I needed a lot of them to last me the night.

It was very peaceful as I sat down on my tarp bed. I focused on the fire and let my senses take in all the sights, sounds and smells. I was hearing things that I had never heard before and frankly sounded prehistoric. My eyes were soft and more focused, like an animal that is watching out for dangers. Despite the light of the fire, I could see clearly all around me. And my nose caught scents that permeated the smoke of the fire. I honestly didn't think I'd sleep at all being as exposed as I was. I gave the fire one more bunch of wood and decided to lie down. I dozed off and was jolted awake; reminded by the fact I was outside with no walls, doors or windows surrounding me. Plus it got cold as the fire died down. I would get up, collect more burning materials and stoke the fire again. It would warm me up just enough and I would doze off again. At one point when I woke up, I peered through the Spanish moss and oak branches right above me. The clarity of the stars was incredible.

After dozing off one last time, instead of being jolted awake, I opened my eyes and noticed that first light was upon us. I stood up, looked east and could see the silhouettes of the trees and buildings start to appear. The sky looked just like it did in my meditations of Zoi at the lake. Deep blue, into pinks, into yellows. I gathered one more batch of wood and stoked the fire again. I had such an appreciation for being there. I looked off into the distance and could see the fires of my other two campmates starting to come to life again.

Despite all of the overnight activity of waking up and stoking the fire, I felt well rested. I hadn't been this connected to nature in a very long time. It was a new day. It made perfect sense that if you let it, Mother Nature will always welcome you back, because that is our nature — to be connected.

We convened at Scott's campsite again for an insanely good breakfast of bacon and eggs, and we recalled our night's experience while we ate. We heard machinery coming toward us and saw an old rusted-out tractor approaching. It was Gary with two of his dogs seated next to him. Gary is a true tribal elder, very connected to his nature and the 400-acre farm. When he asked where I was from, I said Maine. Gary launched into this long story of how his family roots were in Maine. He told us how this farm was purchased by his father and uncle for $25 an acre after the Great Depression. We were engrossed in this story and were only interrupted when one of the dogs tried to eat some eggs from the pan. Gary swatted at the dog and yelled, "Get away from that, you dumbhead!" I think both dogs' names were Dumbhead now that I think about it. Anyway, they respected him. John and I were grateful to Gary for sharing that story and letting us stay on his land. He said we could come back anytime. We were trusted.

John and I spent the remainder of the morning working on our stories with Scott. Being this open and free of distractions, the emotional aspects of our stories came to life. It was incredible what nature can provide you with if you let it.

169

When we packed up the Suburban and headed back out to Highway 39, Scott said that we would almost be offended when we returned to society after this experience. He was right. I didn't turn on my iPhone for another four hours afterward, and only because I had to respond to some email messages. It felt more like a return to a new beginning, to a life of thriving, that I didn't think was possible just three years prior. Just as the previous night gave way to the creation of the new day, so too is the clearer path I still walk on, guided every step of the way. By Zoi.

Conclusion

Grief is one of the hardest journeys to walk in life. We all need guidance through it. I get it. I've walked it, and some of you are walking it now. The thing is, at some point we're all going to be on this path, or know someone who is.

Our greatest strengths arise when we work through our struggles, not go around them or avoid them. They are an inevitable part of life. That, ladies and gentlemen, is the only reason that I wrote this book. I hope that by sharing my experience with you, it will help you build the capacity for your true resilience. Survival is temporary. No matter how high of a performer you are, no matter how tough we believe we are, no matter our background, no matter how much money we have in the bank, people close to us die, traumatic events happen, and life throws us curveballs. The difference is: we can move past surviving and thrive.

Zoi has been my Sherpa, guiding me. And I invite you to take those first steps on your journey to walk through your grief, work through your struggles and live with intention. My promise to you is that if you do this work, you will have a toolset to not just survive, but to thrive because of it. What commitment to your future self *will* you make today?

Sending love to you all. Just be.

Eric Hodgdon

References

Chapter 3

http://www.huffingtonpost.com/william-b-bradshaw/died-passed-away-or-passed_b_6240282.html

Chapter 22

https://www.forbes.com/sites/davidkwilliams/2015/05/07/returning-to-work-after-the-devastating-loss-of-a-loved-one/#4caaa3fe6900

Chapter 32

https://www.forbes.com/sites/alicegwalton/2015/02/09/7-ways-meditation-can-actually-change-the-brain/#650f95f81465

http://www.yalescientific.org/2012/05/the-healing-art-of-meditation/

http://health.usnews.com/wellness/mind/articles/2016-12-08/mindfulness-in-schools-when-meditation-replaces-detention

About the author

Eric Hodgdon is a speaker and trainer, and a warrior for resilience in memory of his dynamic daughter, Zoi. After losing Zoi in early 2014 to suicide, Eric vowed to fight for his family and all of his daughter's friends to find a pathway back to better days.

Eric trains resilience leaders and others who are stuck in grief and struggle to raise their frequency and rise above the noise, so they may thrive and see the beauty in life again.

Eric lives in the Boston area with his rescue dog, Bean.

Eric's email is: eric@erichodgdon.com

Eric Hodgdon Speaking Topics

Since the loss of his daughter Zoi, Eric has been gifted with the opportunity to get in front of tens of thousands of kids, parents, school counselors, mental health professionals, doctors, corporate leaders and working professionals to help them build resilience — to move past surviving to thrive in life. Below are some of Eric's most popular speeches.

Through Struggle We Build Strength Keynote

Eric has given this speech to students, parents, school administrators and mental health professionals in several settings, both in person and live online. The dynamic message in this talk is that working through our own struggles gives us strength to become resilient.

The 3 Best Ways to Build Resilience

The pre-interview has become the most watched video for the inaugural Single Parent Summit. In this personal yet inspirational talk, Eric shares his own journey of divorce and the value of building resilience in any family setting despite the inevitable struggles of life.

Navigating Struggles in the Workplace

Understanding struggle in the workplace isn't easy. This powerful talk is designed for employees, business leaders, and employers who are looking for ways to bridge the gap between struggle and productivity. Eric shares his four-step process for not only navigating struggles, but also gives the framework for resolution.

RESOURCES

WEBSITES:

National Suicide Prevention Lifeline:

1-800-273-8255

https://suicidepreventionlifeline.org

There are always options! If someone you know is struggling emotionally or having a hard time, you can be the difference in getting them the help they need. It's important to take care of yourself when you are supporting someone through a difficult time, as this may stir up difficult emotions. If it does, please reach out for support yourself.

www.erichodgdon.com

New website with free resources like weekly video blog posts, downloads like MAPS worksheets and the 30-day Gratitude journal, info on how to work with Eric, upcoming workshop events, and opportunities to see Eric speak.

www.activeminds.org

Download a copy of *One Hundred Thousand Voices*.

Recording artist Marissa Nadler, a former art teacher for Zoi, had been asked to contribute to an album called *One Hundred Thousand Voices*, all proceeds from which go to www.activeminds.org. Active Minds is the leading nonprofit organization that empowers students to speak openly about mental health, to educate others and encourage people to seek help. Marissa's song is called "Carnival."

www.mannup.com

Former Green Beret (Ret.) Lt. Col. Scott Mann is an expert on 'rooftop leadership' and helping veterans transition into civilian life. A speaker, author and one of my mentors, Scott's teaches rooftop leadership to civilians like me. Rooftop leadership is a set of specialized skills that allows you to make an impact with a purpose that is much bigger than you, and it inspires people to follow you not because they have to, but because they choose to. Scott launched his other mission, www.theheroesjourney.org to help transitioning veterans find their voice through story, so that this becomes their biggest asset as they move from active military duty to the civilian world.

www.BoEason.com

Former NFL pro turned playwright turned professional speaker Bo Eason helps you build your personal story to the benefit of others. In Bo's sessions, you learn why being vulnerable is crucial to telling a personal story. And when your story is personal, it becomes universal. His 'pull no punches' approach to working with players only ensures that you're in the right place, at the right time, with the right people to make your voice be heard.

Books I recommend:

Proof of Heaven, Dr. Eben Alexander

Tribe, Sebastian Junger

Mission America, Scott Mann

The War of Art , Steven Pressfield

Turning Pro, Steven Pressfield

The Warrior Ethos, Steven Pressfield

Social media:

www.facebook.com/GetUp8

www.instagram.com/ericbhodgdon

Made in United States
North Haven, CT
01 May 2023